A Guide to the Basque Country

Five Walking Tours

P S Quick

Published in 2020 by
Acorn Books
www.acornbooks.co.uk

Acorn Books is an imprint of
Andrews UK Limited
www.andrewsuk.com

Copyright © 2020 PS Quick

The right of PS Quick to be identified as the author of this work has been asserted in accordance with the Copyright, Designs and Patents Act 1988.

All rights reserved. No part of this publication may be reproduced, stored in any retrieval system or transmitted in any form or by any means, electronic, mechanical, photocopying, recording or otherwise, without the prior written permission of the copyright holder for which application should be addressed in the first instance to the publishers. No liability shall be attached to the author, the copyright holder or the publishers for loss or damage of any nature suffered as a result of the reliance on the reproduction of any of the contents of this publication or any errors or omissions in the contents.

All information used within this book is believed to be correct at the time of writing. If you find any information within this book that has changed, please advise the publisher who will be happy to correct it in future editions.

Maps included courtesy of openstreetmap.org

Contents

Introduction v
Preparation vi

The First Tour: Bayonne 1
The Second Tour: Biarritz 25
The Third Tour: Hendaye 45
The Fourth Tour: Hondarribia 61
The Fifth Tour: San Sebastián 78

Final Thoughts 100

Eglise Sainte-Eugénie, Biarritz

Introduction

The Basque Country of France and Spain known locally as *Euskadi Herria* has a unique identity with its own culture and language. Offering spectacular scenery, old and modern architecture, a rich history, traditions and gastronomy it is a wonderful place to visit.

This book aims to give the tourist an opportunity to visit and enjoy not only the few major attractions that a guided tour usually includes but many of the other interesting sights that many people do not see. By providing five different walking routes and detailed information about each attraction passed it puts a visitor to the Basque Country in charge of the time spent at any particular place rather than having to rush and keep up with a guide or join costly tours.

The tours will enable you to compare five contrasting destinations in the Basque Country. Enjoy the Belle Époque architecture of San Sebastián with its sandy beaches made famous by Queen Maria Cristina or the stylish town of Biarritz frequented by Napoleon and Eugénie. Visit the towns of Hendaye and Hondarribia to see how the tensions between France and Spain affected these towns located on opposite sides of the River Bidasoa. Wander along the riverbanks of Bayonne lined with the half-timbered buildings or explore its fortifications.

Preparation

- The climate in the Basque Country is generally temperate and warm although rainfall is significant even during the driest month. On the coast summer temperatures average 19°C and winter 9°C although these can vary considerably. Always take a waterproof jacket. July and August are the best times to visit but resorts are crowded at this time.

- The Basque Country has a number of festivals and celebrations. If you enjoy pomp and ceremony check online to confirm the festival dates as they vary from year to year. Hotels will be more expensive at these times.

- Ask at your hotel for a city map and other tourist information. Failing this visit a tourist office as soon as you can on arrival to pick up details of attractions and opening times together with a large free map which is essential in order to get your bearings and understand where places are located. Many tourist offices also have detailed maps that you can download from the internet.

- Do your research and read through this guide in order to decide which museums or other places you want to go into before leaving home. The Basque country has some excellent museums that reflect its history and cultural heritage. Many are closed on certain days of the week or have reduced opening hours. Because times change checking online will give you the latest information.

- Local transport in the towns is varied but all have bus services. However you will absorb the atmosphere of the places in this guide if you can walk around the sites. Many of the towns now also have cycles for hire. Some of these tours involve quite a lot of walking so consider staying overnight and splitting the tour into two days or take a bus back at the end of the tour.

- Although you could learn a few French or Spanish words and local people are extremely friendly, be aware that in these towns some people only speak the Basque language. Taking a phrase book could be useful. Print out your travel details to show people in case there is a problem.

The Tours

The First Tour: Bayonne

The pretty city of Bayonne stretches along the banks of the rivers Ardour and Nive, its buildings decorated with a mix of French and Basque architecture, all adorned with colourful wooden shutters.

There is evidence of a settlement here since ancient times. The Romans came to the city in the first century and surrounded it with a city wall to keep out invaders. When they left in the fourth century the Basques who had always been present became dominant again.

As the capital of the French Basque Country Bayonne has been a strategic stronghold since medieval times and many of the old ramparts are still visible as you walk around the city. It is a joy to explore its shady cobbled streets, riverside quays, pretty half-timbered buildings and its plethora of restaurants.

Bayonne has good transport links which include trains, buses, coaches and the nearby Biarritz-Anglet-Bayonne Airport. The airport is seven kilometres away and has a bus connecting it to Bayonne every half hour although this is less frequent on Sundays and public holidays. San Sebastián/Hondarribia airport is forty kilometres away and Bilbao 155 kilometres away but there is no direct transport link from these to Bayonne.

The train station is located in the Saint-Esprit neighbourhood just across the Saint-Esprit Bridge. The TGV that runs between Paris and Hendaye stops here. There are also other regional train services along the Basque coast.

The bus station is located at Plaza Pio XII with buses to nearby cities. There is a free electric shuttle bus that runs from the city gates to the parks and streets of the central district. Buses that run within the town are cheap and can also be bought as part of the Bayonne City Pass.

There are cycle paths located along the bank of the River Nive and other parts of the city. The city offers free bicycles on loan. It is possible to enjoy a river trip which explores the Adour and its tributaries from February to December.

Bayonne is famous throughout the world for its spectacular summer festival known as *Les fêtes de Bayonne*. There are other cultural, traditional, sporting or gastronomic events held here during the year. Over Easter the market and the river banks of the Nive host displays of the best hams while during the Feast of the Ascension weekend there is chocolate making and tasting.

There are three main areas of Bayonne. Grand Bayonne is the ancient heart of the city and the more commercial part. It is separated from the more traditional Basque quarter by the River Nive. These two areas which are both part of France's Basque region are separated from the Saint-Esprit district, originally part of Gascony, by the River Adour. Connecting these districts there are a number of bridges.

The Tour begins at the confluence of the Nive and Adour rivers at Bayonne City Hall and finishes in the Saint-Esprit district, having explored the three main areas of Bayonne. Bayonne is well known for its ham and chocolate so a visit to see how these are made is included in the tour.

First Tour: Main Sights

- Mairie de Bayonne
- Bartizan on the Réduit
- La Citadelle
- Jardins René Cassin and Léon Bonnat
- Memorial aux Bayonnais Morts
- Jardin Botanique
- Porte de la Poterne
- Château Vieux
- Rue Port Neuf
- Cathédrale Sainte-Marie de Bayonne
- Place Pasteur
- Rue and Porte d'Espagne
- Rue de Salt, La Plachotte and Tour de Salt
- Pont du Génie
- La Jambon de Bayonne
- Château Neuf
- Église Saint André
- La Trinquet Saint André
- Musée Basque and Musée Bonnat-Helleu
- Pont Saint-Esprit
- Gare de Bayonne
- L'Atelier du Chocolat

Grand Bayonne – Part 1

Grand Bayonne

La Mairie de Bayonne

The impressive Bayonne City Hall, known as *La Mairie* or *L'Hotel de Ville* is a Neo-Classical building located at the confluence of the Nive and Adour rivers. With a view of both rivers its position was ideal for monitoring the maritime activity of this Basque cultural capital.

Today the building houses the administration offices, a theatre and a café with terrace. It is the centre point for the Bayonne festivals and summer gatherings. When it was built in 1842–3 to the plans drawn up by Charles Vionnois it was originally home to the Customs Office. Since then the building has had other functions such as a Library, an Archive Centre, a Museum of Culture and also a Painting Museum.

If you are in Bayonne at the end of July and beginning of August look up to the balcony to see a representation of *King Leo*, a reference to Leon Dacharry, an opera singer who became the mascot of Bayonne. He reigns there until the end of festivities on the Sunday evening.

On close inspection the building has a number of interesting features. The peristyle arcades reflect the old canal architecture of the Rue Port Neuf which is nearby. The Bayonne Coat of Arms inspired by the seal of 1351 and a keystone of the city can be found on the forecourt of the Town Hall. It is said to represent the *pride of the people* and *a city never soiled*. The red blazon of the coat of arms portrays life and a desire to serve one's country with green oaks that symbolise power and regeneration.

On the coat of arms are two golden lions trying to seize a crenelated golden tower which represent the English and the French trying to capture the city of Bayonne. The Fleur de Lys symbolises French Royalty while the crown above refers to the Saint-Esprit district attached to the city.

Perched on the roof of the Town Hall, looking out across Bayonne since 1842, there are six statues that represent the economic and artistic activities of the city. From left to right these are Navigation, Industry, Art, Commerce, Astronomy and Agriculture. Originally created from faux stone and badly deteriorated by the weather these statues were replaced by iron ones in 1891 when the Town Hall was restored after a devastating fire.

From the City Hall walk south-east on Rue Bernède towards the river onto Place de la Liberté and Quai Amiral Lespes. From here you can see the Bartizan on the Réduit.

Bartizan on the Réduit

As you walk along the river bank look across and you will see the Bartizan on the Réduit which is the overhanging corner turret built on the river battlements. Standing at the end of the Saint-Esprit Bridge it was designed by Vauban in 1680 and built in the late seventeenth century.

The destruction of the Réduit was ordered so that the traffic would flow more freely. The Porte of France that stood here was dismantled in 1907. The dismantled stones were used to raise the esplanade and the statue of Cardinal Lavigerie that stands here today was erected in 1909. Part of the Réduit door was reinstalled at the Poterne in 1993. The watchtower collapsed into the Adour in 1937 but was restored in 2005.

Bayonne City Hall with the Bartizan on the Réduit in the foreground

Continue walking along Quai Amiral Lespes onto Avenue du Maréchal Leclerc for 200 metres. Stop opposite Place Charles de Gaulle. Look across the river to see Bayonne Citadel.

La Citadelle de Bayonne

There is a good view of the Bayonne Citadel rising above the town from the banks of the River Adour. The premises are now occupied by the Military and not regularly open to the general public. In 1750 a garrison of two thousand men was stationed at the Citadel. It last saw action at the end of the Peninsular War when it was taken by General Hill.

The Citadel was designed by Vauban in the seventeenth century on a square design with four bastions. Vauban was a French military engineer who was commissioned as a Marshal of France. He was renowned for his skill in designing fortifications and breaking through them as well as advising Louis XIV on how to make France's borders more defensible.

Cross the road onto Place Charles de Gaulle. Walk 50 metres. The Gardens of René Cassin and Léon Bonnat will be on the right.

Jardin René Cassin

The Garden of René Cassin is named after the former First World War soldier René Cassin, a French lawyer who founded the Union Fédérale. He was awarded the Nobel Peace Prize in 1968 for his work drafting the Universal Declaration of Human Rights.

This irregular shaped rustic garden is filled with perennials, grasses and trees. A fountain sits in the heart of the garden and there are two impressive Magnolias. In spring and summer the air is filled with perfume from its flowers.

Jardin Léon Bonnat

The Garden of Léon Bonnat remembers the French painter who was born in Bayonne. He was also a Grand Officer of the Légion d'honneur and professor at the École des Beaux Arts.

The garden designed in a classic French style was created in 1907 and the original wrought iron fence remains today. Its symmetry is in direct contrast to the garden of René Cassin. The edges of the garden comprise a collection of annuals, biennials, perennials and shrubs while in the centre there is a large pond and fountain.

Leave the gardens, walk north-west on Avenue Léon Bonnat, turn left onto Place de Basques. The Tourist Office will be on the right.

Office de Tourisme de Bayonne

Call in at the Tourist Office to pick up a large scale map of the city together with opening times of museums and other attractions.

Continue south-west on Place des Basques for 150 metres. Cross Avenue du 11 Novembre 1918 onto the Esplanade de Verdun. The War Memorial will be ahead.

Memorial aux Bayonnais Morts

Located on the Esplanade de Verdun the limestone Bayonne War Memorial pays tribute to the eight hundred soldiers who died for France in the First World War. The monument was financed by the local population in 1920. Since then it has also been dedicated to the dead of other wars.

The memorial sits against the ramparts and comprises two figures framing the list of the dead. One of the figures is a Basque herdsman with his ox which symbolises life which the other is a soldier and his rifle.

From the Esplanade de Verdun you can access the Botanic Garden.

Jardin Botanique

The Botanical Garden sits seven metres above the seventeenth century city ramparts facing the Cathedral. In this small space many different landscapes have been created that are filled with a thousand different varieties of plants and trees, all clearly labelled. The centrepiece is a beautiful garden designed in a Japanese style.

The enchanting walkway takes you over the water on a bright red Japanese bridge. Stand on the bridge and admire the waterfall or the carp and turtles swimming below then look across the rest of the garden. Rest in the hanging garden or continue to stroll and enjoy the maples, banana trees, agapanthus, bamboo, dodecatheon, peonies and other varieties that fill your senses with their colours and perfumes.

After exploring the garden walk towards the city wall and follow it round until you reach the Porte de la Poterne.

Porte de la Poterne

On the east side of the Botanical gardens you will see the Postern Gate leading through the battlements to the Château Vieux. The entrance is also known as La Poterne. It was pierced through the ramparts in the nineteenth century to give access to Château Vieux through a thirty metre long tunnel.

This tunnel has gates on both sides. One gives access inside the city to the Château Vieux while the other leads to the gardens of the Poterne on the outside. The seventeenth century Porte du Réduit was dedicated to Hercules, god of armies and agriculture. The newer lighter door that is slightly offset from the wall was one of the original doors of the Réduit and was placed here in 1993.

Walk east on Allée de la Poterne onto Rue des Gouverneurs. The Château Vieux will be on the left.

Château Vieux

The Château Vieux, also known as the Castillo Viejo, is a medieval castle built in the eleventh century by the Viscounts of Labourd on the site of a Roman castrum or military camp which housed the garrison and administration of the *Lapurdum* region. The building was originally the official residence of the governors of the city including the English Black Prince Edward.

The castle took the name of Château Vieux at the end of the fifteenth century when a new castle was built in the Petit-Bayonne district. In line with his other work in the city Vauban fortified the castle destroying the dungeon but adding a fortified forecourt so that it became the north-west support point. It was classed as an historic monument in 1931 and has always been the seat of the city's military authorities. Today it is still owned by the army.

Continue along Rue des Gouverneurs for 60 metres onto Rue Thiers, turn right after 45 metres onto Rue des Carmes then right onto Rue Port Neuf. Walk 65 metres onto Rue de la Monnaie. After 100 metres the Cathedral will be straight ahead.

Rue Port Neuf

The slight detour to the route was made to see this street with its attractive arcades. This road was formerly a canal.

Cathédrale Sainte-Marie de Bayonne

Dominating the skyline and situated on a mound overlooking the Nive and Adour rivers the Gothic Cathedral of Saint Mary of Bayonne with its strong Champagne influence was built from locally sourced red and white stone. Construction began in the early thirteenth century, though the cathedral was only completed in the seventeenth. The two spires were erected in the nineteenth century; at the same time the building was restored and refurbished by Émile Boeswildwald.

Bayonne Cathedral

The cathedral was the seat of the former Bishops of Bayonne, built on the site of a Romanesque cathedral destroyed by the fires of 1258 and 1310. Bayonne Cathedral is on the Camino de Santiago route which joins the *Camino del Norte* in Irún, Spain. This route was used by pilgrims on their way to Santiago de Compostela.

Both the exterior and interior offer a host of rich architectural treasures to be enjoyed. The adjoining Gothic cloister dating back to 1240 is one of the largest in France. In the Middle Ages this cloister was a cemetery and also a place of deliberation.

The statues that once stood in the niches of the west porch are no longer there because they were demolished during the Revolution. Above the porch is a rose window and surmounting this is the shield of France carried by two angels.

The nave is 26 metres high and above it runs the triforium, a gallery that goes all around the building. In the first bay of the nave look out for the three lions on the keystone that represent the Kings of England. The beautiful stained glass windows of the Renaissance period were restored in the nineteenth century and show scenes from Genesis and the Gospels. The mahogany pulpit with its spectacular sculptures dates from 1760.

The oldest part of the building where the Champagne influence is most evident is the chorus and deambulatory. The choir has six cylindrical pillars and there are five polygonal chapels and two quadrangular ones connected by a walkway with paintings to view. A crypt containing the tombs of bishops is located under the choir.

On the left is the chapel of Saint John the Baptist with his symbol the eagle on the keystone. There is a magnificent stained glass window in the chapel of Saint Jerome that dates back to 1531. A statue of Joan of Arc can be found in the penultimate chapel and the last chapel of the Baptismal Fonts built by the Laduch family to house the family tomb has a flamboyant Gothic window.

On the right hand side by the west porch behind the second door is a seventeenth century chapel with a vault and an elaborate window. Behind the passage leading to the cloister, part of which was demolished in order to build it last century, is the chapel of the martyr Saint Leon who was the first Bishop of Bayonne. In the transept above the sacristy is the sixteenth century keystone which represents a Bayonne ship and its crew, remembering a time when the port of Bayonne traded with Spain, Flanders and England.

Walk around the back of the Cathedral to Place Pasteur.

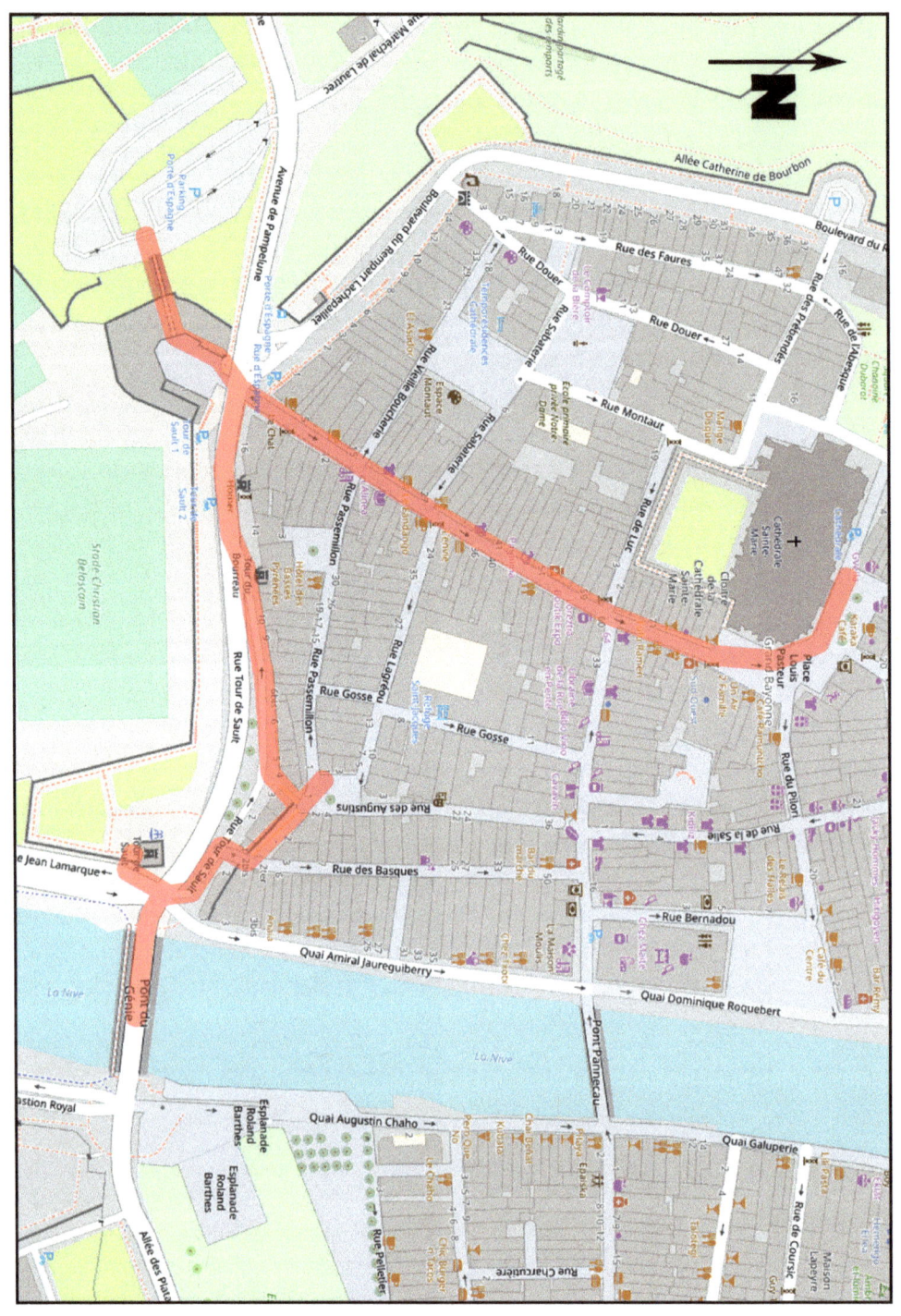

Grand Bayonne – Part 2

Place Pasteur

Behind Bayonne Cathedral is Place Pasteur where the old pillory and gallows once stood. The stone fountain located here has four bronze masks cast in the shape of lion heads. There are cafes in this area to rest and watch the world go by.

Walk south on Place Pasteur onto Rue d'Espagne for 220 metres. Cross the road to see the Gate of Spain.

Rue and Porte d'Espagne

Rue d'Espagne was the main Roman road that led down to the Gate of Spain, an important entry gate to the city in mediaeval times. This street was once two streets. One was called Tendes Street named after the tents erected here during the times when markets were held and the other was Mayou Street which was the main street of the time. The town prison was originally located in the two towers of Mignon at its southern end but these towers have since been demolished. Today this busy street is pedestrianised and filled with shops and cafes.

At the end of the street look up at the buildings on each side and you will see the remaining parts of the old city walls of *Lapurdun* which was the name of the old Roman settlement. Across the road you will see the Gate of Spain which for two centuries was the only exit from the south of the city. In the Middle Ages it was protected by a barbican while in the seventeenth century the defences were strengthened by the addition of casemates and a drawbridge. By the beginning of the twentieth century it was obvious that this gate was too narrow to allow vehicles through so in 1914 a wider entrance was made nearby.

Turn left onto Rue de Salt. Just before this road ends turn left onto Passage de la Pusterle then immediately up the steps of Rue Passemillon where you will find La Plachotte.

Rue d'Espagne city wall and gate with watchtower

Rue de Salt, La Plachotte and Tour de Salt

Following the Rue de Salt you will see the fourth century watchtowers built into the old city walls between the houses. Climbing the steps from Passage de la Pusterle to Rue Passemillon you will arrive at the Plachotte with its northern tower and the wall of the Roman enclosure, also from the fourth century.

Here where the restoration of Bayonne began you can enjoy a splendid mixture of architecture from different centuries. As well as the Roman period there are the beautiful restored houses from the seventeenth and eighteenth centuries. The traditional colours of blue, green and red are a symbol of the town.

Retrace steps back to the Rue de Salt then cross the road to see the Tour de Salt and the Genie Bridge.

Le Pont du Génie

The Genie Bridge with its three arches replaced the old boom barring the entrance to the River Nive. The stone bridge replaced the first wooden one that dated from 1799. Stand on the bridge and look along the river in both directions for wonderful views of Bayonne and the houses built along the quays.

The buildings display a mix of Basque and French architecture adorned with their wooden shutters. Along the quays on both sides of the Nive River there are cafes, bars and restaurants. Wander into the side streets and you will find even more.

Quai Amiral Jaureguiberry, Grand Bayonne

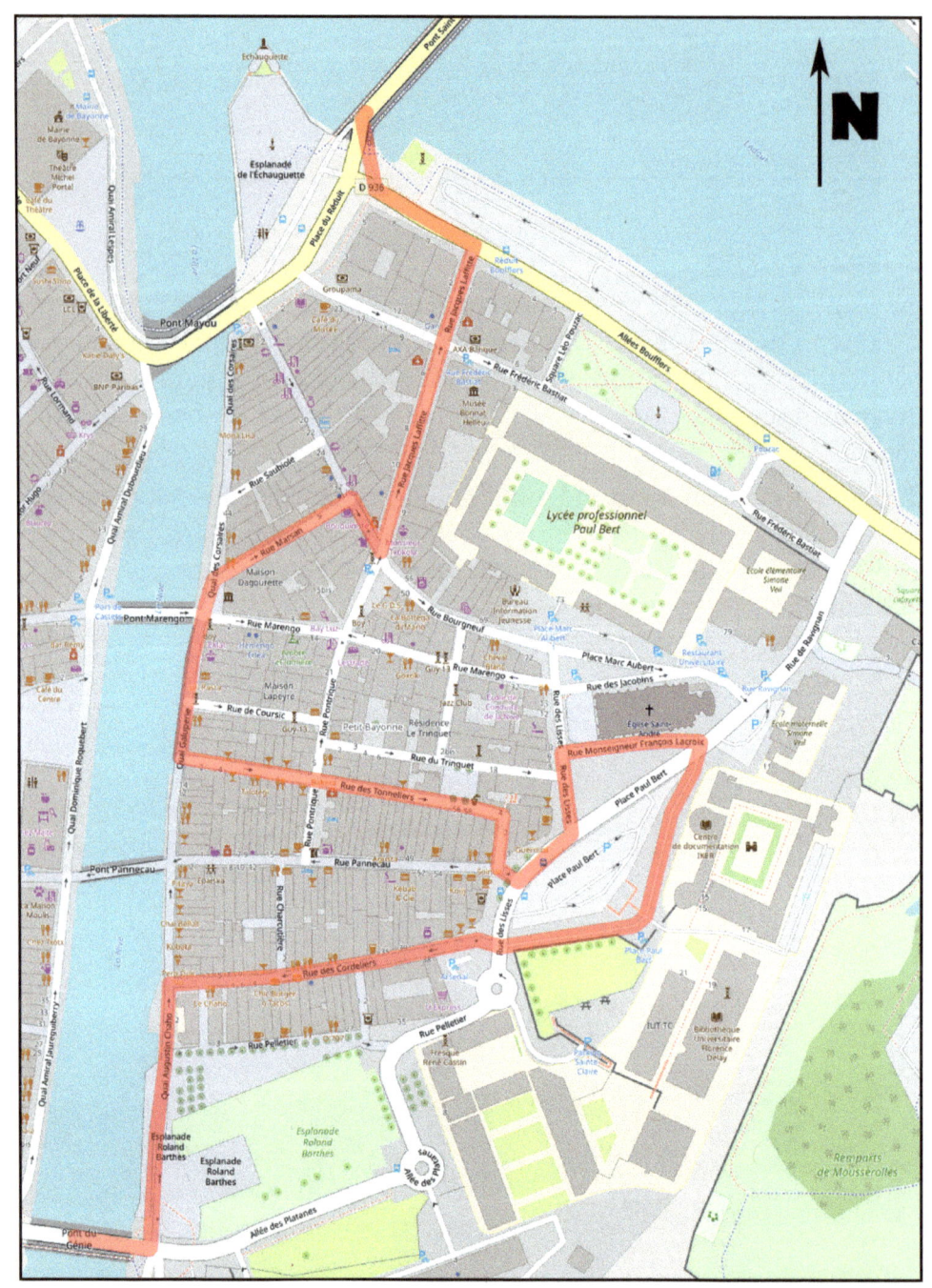

Petit Bayonne

Petit Bayonne

Cross the bridge to Petit Bayonne. Turn left along the river onto Quai Augustin Chaho for 130 metres. Turn right onto Rue des Cordeliers. The famous ham shop is on the left after 150 metres.

La Jambon de Bayonne

Bayonne Ham is a famous regional cured ham which has been associated with the town since the Middle Ages when it was exported from the port of Bayonne. Every year it is celebrated at the Easter Trade Fair.

In the Pierre Ibaialde shop at 41 Rue des Cordeliers you can find out how this ham is produced and also taste samples of the ham and other specialities. The ham is produced from one of eight clearly defined breeds of pig under strict regulations which include the area where the pigs are raised and the feeding regime.

Continue east along Rue des Cordeliers for 45 metres onto Place Paul Bert. The Château Neuf will be on the right after 120 metres.

Château Neuf

The New Castle was designed by the same architect responsible for Caernarfon Castle in Wales. It was first built as a town gateway by Edward I, King of England. Then in the fifteenth century at the end of the Hundred Years' War Charles VII completed the work. It became known as the New Castle to distinguish it from the older castle, the Château Vieux.

The building reveals the influence of British architecture due to the presence of English troops here in earlier times. The fortress was flanked by large powerful towers and in 2010 elements of it were restored. Today it belongs to the University of Bayonne and is closed to the public. The Château Neuf de Bayonne also houses the administration of the Basque Museum.

Walk north on Place Paul Bert for 65 metres then use the zebra crossing to reach the Church of Saint Andrew on Rue Mgr François Lacroix.

Église Saint André

The Church of Saint Andrew built in Neo-Gothic style in the nineteenth century is located next to the Château Neuf. The original towers that formed part of the building were later dismantled as they were too heavy for the foundations. It is well worth a visit to admire the architecture both inside and out.

Above the main door on the exterior you will see a beautiful rose window while inside the painting by Bayonne's own artist Léon Bonnat depicts the Assumption. If you are here on a Sunday join the congregation to listen to a Mass in the Basque language.

Walk west on Rue Mgr François Lacroix for 50 metres, turn left onto Rue des Lisses for 45 metres, turn right to stay on this road. After 40 metres turn right onto Rue du Jeu de Paume. The pelota hall is at the end of the road.

La Trinquet Saint André

The sixteenth century pelota hall located in Rue du Jeu de Paume is the oldest in the world. It has its roots in a very old game known as the *game of palm*. Although the game was abandoned by many it is still popular in the Basque Country. Pelota comes from the Basque word meaning ball. It is possible to watch a game of pelota here every Thursday at 16:00.

Turn onto Rue des Tonneliers. Continue for 200 metres until you reach Quai Galuperie. Turn right, walk 80 metres, continue onto Quai des Corsaires. The Basque Museum will be on the right after 20 metres.

Musée Basque

The Basque Museum is housed in a late sixteenth century trader's house, known as the *Maison Dagourette* . Founded in 1922 it is the most important cultural museum in the Basque country. It was named as *Museum of France* in 2003. There are over two thousand objects housed in twenty thematic rooms spread over three levels.

It is an interesting museum with exhibits relating to the Basque culture as well as the story of Bayonne and its port. It includes such things as information about the everyday lives of shepherds and farmers, paintings, art works, games, and dances from early times through the centuries to the present. It explains why the architecture of Basque houses differs according to their province. As well as the permanent exhibits there are also temporary exhibitions.

Walk south for 20 metres, turn left onto Rue Marsan, right after 90 metres onto Rue Bourgneuf, sharp left after 35 metres onto Rue Jacques Laffitte. The Fine Arts Museum will be on the right after 100 metres.

Musee Bonnat-Helleu

The Bayonne Museum of Fine Arts is named after Léon Bonnat, the local realist painter whose generosity enabled it to be established in this specially designed nineteenth century building. As well as a large number of works by Bonnat the museum also houses works by Rubens, Van Dyck, El Greco, Ribera, Murillo, Leonardo da Vinci, Michelangelo, Goya, Rembrandt, Poussin, Ingres, Delacroix, Géricault, Degas, Barye and Helleu.

The museum has around seven thousand works of art which include not only paintings but sculptures, medals, photographs, drawings, furniture, objects d'art and archaeological objects from ancient times to the present day.

Pont Saint-Esprit

The Holy Spirit Bridge was originally a wooden structure built around 1150. Since then a number of bridges have been damaged by floods and wind. In 1791 nineteen of the twenty-three arches were damaged so a bridge of boats was used to join Bayonne and the suburb of Saint-Esprit until a new bridge could be built.

Construction of the present bridge was started in 1846 and completed in 1849. It was originally named Nemours Bridge in honour of Louis of Orleans who was the sixth Duke of Nemours and laid the first stone. It is a beautiful bridge that has seven arches and is two hundred metres long. In 2010 the bridge was expanded to allow the passage of a tramway. Stand on the bridge for excellent views up and downstream as well as the Saint-Esprit district with the Citadel and Bayonne with the Cathedral in the background.

Walk north for 80 metres onto Rue Jacques Laffitte then turn left. Walk 50 metres, turn right to stay on this road then slight right onto Pont Saint-Esprit.

Holy Spirit Bridge with Cathedral on right and Petit Bayonne on left

Saint-Esprit

21

Saint-Esprit

Crossing the Pont Saint-Esprit you arrive in the suburb of Saint-Esprit or the Holy Spirit neighbourhood. It was originally part of Gascony and very different from the other areas of Bayonne. The first people to settle here were the monks of the Hospital Order of the Holy Spirit who opened a hospice on the roads of Saint-Jacques-de-Compostela, giving the district its name.

It was also the district where the Jews escaping from the Spanish Inquisition settled. These Jews contributed greatly to the growth of Bayonne, especially with the introduction of chocolate at the beginning of the seventeenth century. Others were apothecaries, ship-owners or traders who integrated with the Bayonne population. After the revolution these families of Portuguese and Spanish origin were considered citizens.

Cross the bridge then continue 50 metres onto Republic Square.

Place de la République

Republic Square is a height of activity with its cafes and shops. Located here is a stone fountain with a hexagonal basin and a monolithic column. It is decorated with cast iron elements; a representation of a dolphin on each side and a vase at the top with six sconces.

The fountain was erected in 1860. At the bottom is the signature of the sculptor J J Ducel. The fountain is fed by water from Mont Ursuya although for centuries legend stated that its source was the Holy Spirit.

From this square you can see the Holy Spirit Church and the railway station.

Walk north-west across the square and you will see the Church of the Holy Spirit ahead.

Église Saint-Esprit

The Church of the Holy Spirit was built on the foundations of a Romanesque priory. Some of these elements can still be seen in the church today. Constructed in the fifteenth century on orders from Louis XI it contains the relics of Saint Irene. The beautiful Gothic vaults of the choir are decorated with interlacing flamboyant medallions. There is also a stunning polychrome portraying the Virgin Mary on a donkey which symbolizes the flight into Egypt.

Walk to the roundabout then turn left to view the station.

Gare de Bayonne

The railway line arrived from Paris in 1854 bringing tourists to enjoy the beaches of Biarritz and surrounding area. Today Bayonne railway station is served by TGV, Intercités and TER services operated by the SNCF. If you have not arrived in Bayonne by train it is worth a visit to see this charming building with its arches and clock tower.

Gare de Bayonne

Walk north-east past the station on Rue Maubec for 80 metres. The synagogue will be on the left.

Synagogue

The synagogue in Rue Maubec was opened in 1837 and is evidence of the Jewish history of this part of Bayonne. It is not open to the public but visits can be made by special reservation.

The chocolate workshop is a 30 minute walk from the station. Catch the A1 or A2 bus here to save time if needed.

To return to Place de la République, head to the Quai Amiral Bergeret, and turn left. Continue for 750 metres, turn left onto Rue des Lavandières for 60 metres, right onto Boulevard Alsace Lorraine which becomes Avenue du Maréchal Juin.

Cross the roundabout, stay on Avenue du Maréchal Juin, turn right after 240 metres onto Avenue de la Division Leclerc, bear right after 210 metres onto Allée de Gibéléou. L'Atelier du Chocolat is number 7.

L'Atelier du Chocolat

A visit to the chocolate workshop belonging to Serge Andrieu provides an opportunity not only to see the confectioners in action and sample the product but also to learn about the history of the cocoa bean and its introduction to Europe through information panels and a film; both of which are available in English.

The Second Tour: Biarritz

Biarritz is a stylish seaside town located on France's south-western Basque coast. Its popularity grew after Napoleon III and his Spanish born wife Eugénie stayed there during the mid-nineteenth century although Victor Hugo had already fallen in love with Biarritz in 1843. Today there is an avenue named after him. The American scriptwriter Peter Viertel came to Biarritz in 1957 with his wife Deborah Kerr to shoot his film *The Sun Also Rises*.

Biarritz was originally a whaling town but with its important European visitors became a fashionable summer resort for the extravagant wealthy aristocrats. It has a stunning coastline and is a popular destination for surfers but additionally has a rich history with eclectic architecture incorporating a mixture of historic styles. With its buildings of historical and artistic value with Belle Époque and Art Deco characteristics it retains some of the glamour of bygone years. A visit to the Grand Hotel du Palais built by Napoleon III for his wife Eugénie bears testament to this.

Biarritz is hilly in parts and if you arrive at the airport or station you will need to get a bus or taxi to take you to your hotel. There is no taxi rank at the station but there are buses that stop outside. It takes about ten minutes in a taxi or forty minutes to walk into the main areas of Biarritz as the railway station is out of town. If you need a taxi you have to ring for a taxi yourself. Plan well ahead too for your homeward journey. It is sometimes impossible to hire a taxi at short notice.

Make sure you ask your hotel for a map of Biarritz and any other information they can give you. There is a tourist office near the City Hall in Square d'Ixelles but it is not easy to find and away from the main attractions. As with the other walks in this book maps have been provided, though a locally-sourced one or those online at http://tourisme.biarritz.fr/en/ documentation may well feature more detail.

There is an open-air tram designed to look like an 1850s train which offers tours of the main sights of Biarritz lasting for thirty minutes. It departs from the Esplanade Casino and also Rocher de la Vierge.

There are six kilometres of beaches in Biarritz that are varied in their size and characteristics. The walk around Biarritz follows these beaches along to the lighthouse visiting local attractions and viewpoints on the way. The return journey takes a route through the town to explore famous buildings and appreciate the history of Biarritz as well as museums and other attractions.

There is a lot of walking if all features are included and visiting all the museums can take a lot of time so the route is planned as a circular one to give you the opportunity to start anywhere and if needed split it over two days. For the last part of the tour it is possible to take a number 10 or 13 bus from Les Halles to cut down on the walking. If you are staying in a different part of town ask your hotel to check which buses go to these attractions if you do not want to walk to them.

The tour begins at Place du Port-Vieux which is the old port of Biarritz where the whaling was centred. In the Middle Ages Biarritz was a port with fishermen renowned for their skill in harpooning whales. The cove was sheltered from the rough sea and the gently sloping shore enabled the whalers to beach the whales on the high tide then wait until the low tide when they cut them up.

Second Tour: Main Sights

- La Plage de Port-Vieux
- Rocher de la Vierge
- Aquarium de Biarritz
- Cloche du Plateau de l'Atalaye
- Port des Pêcheurs
- Église Sainte- Eugénie
- Rocher du Basta
- La Grande Plage
- Casino Barrière
- Plage Miramar
- Faro di Biarritz
- Hôtel du Palais
- Église Orthodoxe
- Chapelle Impériale
- Musee d'Art Oriental Asiatica
- Gare du Midi
- Jardin Publique
- Les Halles Biarritz
- Musée Historique de Biarritz
- Plage de la Côte des Basques
- Planète Musée du Chocolat
- Cité de l'Océan

Plague du Port Vieux with a view of Rocher de la Vierge

Biarritz – Part 1

La Plage de Port-Vieux

The smallest beach in Biarritz is the charming Port-Vieux surrounded by arcades. Located close to the town centre it is ideal for families with young children as the beach is in a rocky cove sheltered from the wind with calm water and ideal swimming conditions. There is a lifeguard during the summer season and a number of restaurants and bars nearby.

There are wonderful views across the bay and beautiful sunsets. From here you can see the *Rocher de la Vierge* and the *Aquarium of Biarritz*.

From the Esplanade du Port-Vieux walk north-west on the Esplanade de la Vierge for 190 metres, turn left onto the Esplanade des Anciens Combattants for 50 metres, turn left onto Passerelle Eiffel to cross the footbridge. The Rocher de la Vierge will be ahead.

Rocher de la Vierge

The *Rock of the Virgin* is connected to the mainland by a bridge commissioned by Napoleon III. It was known as the *Eiffel Bridge* after the architect Gustave Eiffel who built the Eiffel Tower in Paris. The footbridge crosses the water before reaching the 75 metre tunnel carved through the rock known as the *Rock of Atalaye* which was the top of the promontory overlooking the sea. At the end the fishermen were able to watch the whales. Today fantastic views of Biarritz can be enjoyed as well as the mountains of the Spanish Basque country and sweeping views of the Bay of Biscay. The rock topped with a statue of the Virgin Mary has become a symbol of Biarritz.

Retrace your steps across the footbridge, make a slight left onto Esplanade des Anciens Combattants then 50 metres later a sharp left onto Boulevard du Maréchal Leclerc. The Aquarium will be on the right.

Aquarium de Biarritz

Situated in the old harbour the Biarritz Aquarium or Sea Life Centre is housed in a recently modernised and extended Art Deco building that has been open to the public since 1933. Here you can enjoy a fascinating display of ocean life including sharks, rays, seals, coral reef life and a Caribbean lagoon. The museum is open daily from April to October although in other months it has reduced opening times.

The museum has exhibits organised on four floors with over 150 species kept in tanks. The first three floors are dedicated to the flora, fauna and whaling history of the Bay of Biscay. Look out for the conger eels, seahorses, the giant octopus, the green sea turtle and the loggerhead turtle. Browse the displays of model ships, nautical charts and navigational instruments.

On the fourth floor which is home to marine life from the Caribbean, Indo-Pacific and North Atlantic, there is a shark tank with hammerhead, reef and zebra sharks together with barracudas, rays and groupers. You can pick up a starfish or be entertained by the seals being fed before wandering out on the panoramic terrace for a breathtaking view.

It is possible to buy a combined ticket for the aquarium and the *Cité de l'Océan* located on the *Côte des Basques*. There is a free shuttle bus to and from this attraction should you want to visit it. You could combine the last part of the tour with this.

> *Turn right on exit from the aquarium to walk north-east on Boulevard du Maréchal Leclerc for 20 metres. Follow the road round for 140 metres. The Cloche du Plateau de l'Atalaye will be on the left.*

Cloche du Plateau de l'Atalaye

Located on the promontory of Atalaye is the old alarm bell used by the whale fisherman. This promontory acted as an observation post and on rough days the bell was rung as a signal for the perfect time for boats to return to port.

In 1759 a cross was erected here in memory of Captain Berdoulin and his son who were drowned at the foot of Atalaye. It was replaced in 1936 by another on the wishes of the priest Gaston Larre before his death. The present cross dates from 1974.

> *Walk south-west for 28 metres then turn left onto Allée Port des Pêcheurs. Stay on this road until you reach the Fisherman's Port.*

Port des Pêcheurs

The Fisherman's Port is an old enclosed harbour with a pretty seawall used today by small pleasure boats and working trawlers. The tides here are quite dramatic and it is interesting to see the boats coming into port. There are a number of restaurants located in this charming area but there is a steep slope down to reach them. Behind the port you will see the Villa de Goeland. Today a guest house it was once a large and majestic villa.

> *Walk south on Allée Port des Pêcheurs for ten metres, continue onto Descente du Port for 70 metres. Make a sharp left onto Boulevard du Maréchal Leclerc for 140 metres then turn right onto Place Sainte-Eugénie.*

Port des Pêcheurs

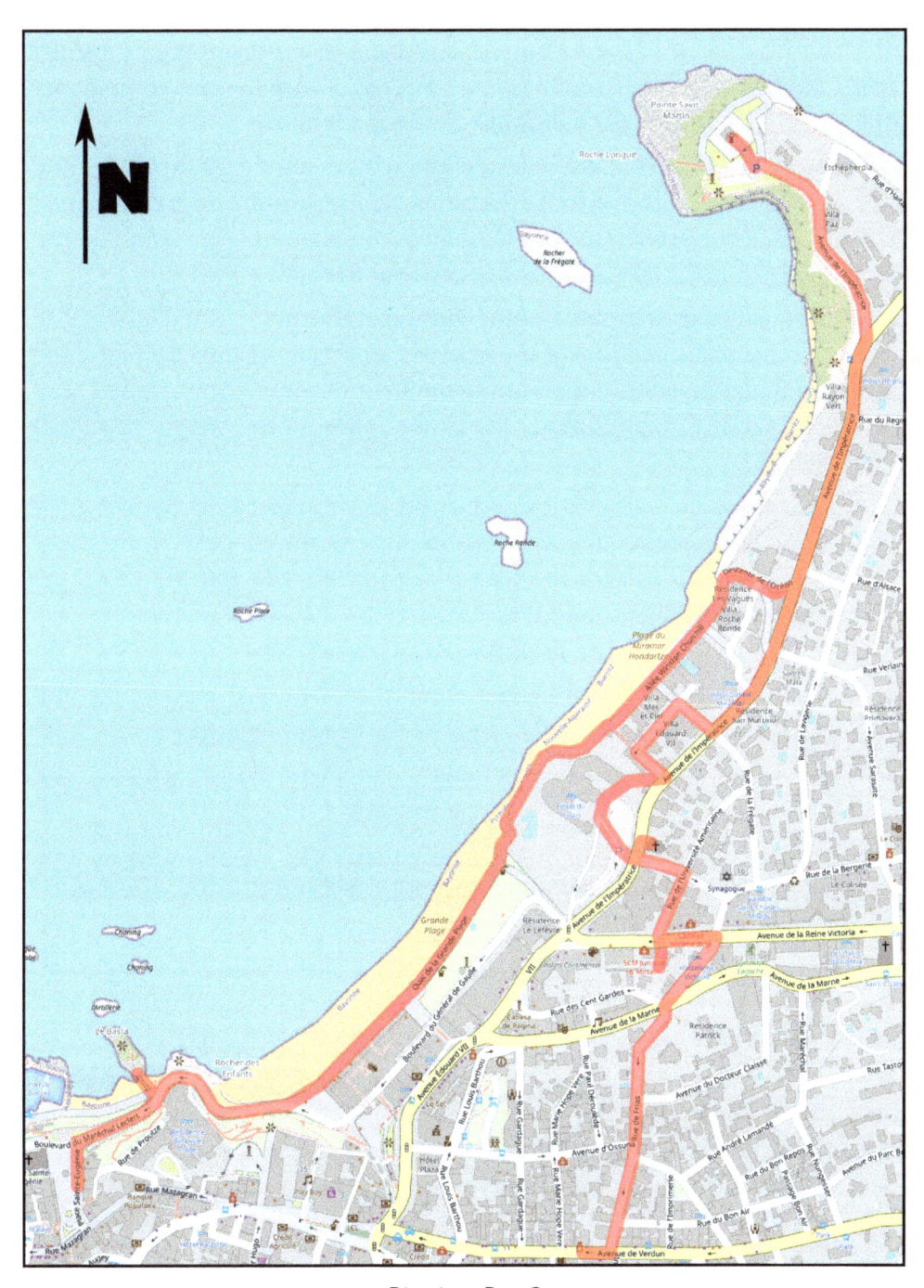

Biarritz – Part 2

Église Sainte-Eugénie

The attractive church of Saint Eugénie is situated in the Place Saint Eugénie, a pretty square with shops, restaurants and hotels. Today the church holds art exhibitions and concerts of traditional and modern music.

Dedicated to Saint Eugénie, the wife of Napoleon III, it is a grey stone building of Neo-Gothic style that overlooks the old port. The church was built between 1898 and 1903 but before that the chapel Notre-Dame-de-Pitié stood on the site. In 1927 the bell tower was constructed and the bells installed in 1931.

Luc-Olivier Merson was responsible for the beautiful stained glass rose windows in the choir and that of the nativity. A parade of saints decorates the walls leading to the altar. Look out for the lily flowers, a pattern often seen which is a Marian symbol linking the consecration to the Virgin Mary and Saint Eugénie.

The tympanum depicts the various saints protecting the city at the centre of Notre Dame du Bon Secours, the original fisherman's chapel. On the right of baby Jesus is Saint Martin the patron saint of Biarritz and the archangel Gabriel while on his left is Saint Eugenie carrying the sword representing his martyrdom and the archangel Michael.

The tomb of the priest Gaston Larre is housed in the crypt. He was the first parish priest and in 1884 decided to modify the original chapel.

> Walk back north on Place Sainte-Eugénie towards the sea then turn right onto Boulevard du Maréchal Leclerc for 110 metres. Cross the Allée Port des Pêcheurs and walk down the steps to the Rocher du Basta.

Rocher du Basta

The Basta rock is a viewpoint from where you have a wonderful panorama of the Bay of Biscay with the beautiful coastline of Biarritz looking back to the Port des Pêcheurs and past the Grand Plage to the lighthouse of Biarritz. There are seats here in this little park to rest and enjoy the view.

> *Retrace your steps to Boulevard du Maréchal Leclercthe, turn left, follow the road round for 30 metres until you come to Boulevard du Général de Gaulle. On this corner is a seating area and viewpoint from where you can see the Grande Plage.*

La Grande Plage

La Grande Plage de Biarritz if the most popular beach for sunbathing and inexperienced surfers. It is the central beach in Biarritz with splendid views of the coast and lighthouse with cafes, restaurants and shops along the promenade or in the nearby lanes. Facing the beach is the *Casino Barrière* while at the far end just before the *Plage du Mirimar* is the *Hôtel du Palais*.

> *Continue south-east on Boulevard du Général de Gaulle until you reach the promenade. The Casino Barrière will be seen on the right facing the sea.*

Casino Barrière

The first casino opened in Biarritz in 1901 but is now a hotel. The present Casino Barrière is an Art Deco building located on the Grande Plage. It was founded in 1912 by François André and restyled in 1929 by the architect Alfred Laulhé.

The casino was modified by the architect Francois Lombard in 1992 to provide new modern public spaces by renovating the facades and interiors. Over the years many famous artists have been welcomed by the casino. These include Edith Piaf, Yves Montand and Charles Trenet. As well as the casino the building is home to a bar, brasserie and live entertainment centre.

> *Continue to follow the promenade, the Quai de la Grande Plage, until you come to the Allée Winston Churchill. You will see the Hôtel du Palais but it cannot be accessed from this side.*

La Grande Plage and La Plage Miramar

La Plage Miramar

La Grande Plage becomes the Plage Miramar as you walk through the walkway located underneath the Hôtel du Palais. This charming beach is more tranquil although when the sea is rough there can be strong currents and so surfing is not permitted.

> *Walk as far as you can along the seafront, turn right to take the Descente de l'Océan for 100 metres. Turn left onto Avenue de l'Impératrice then after 500 metres a slight left onto the Esplanade Elisabeth II. The lighthouse will be ahead.*

Faro di Biarritz

Biarritz lighthouse sits on the Pointe Saint-Martin cliff, a rocky outcrop at the end of the Plage Mirimar. The lighthouse was built between 1830 and 1834. It is 73 metres tall and although sunk into the subsoil does lean slightly. It overlooks Cape Hainsart which was named after the oak trees that originally grew here. Today these have been replaced by tamarisks.

If you want to reach the top of the lighthouse there are 248 steps to climb but the panorama of the Basque coast, Pyrenees and ocean is well worth it on a sunny day. Because there is limited space on the narrow stairs and balcony be prepared to queue on busy days. A visit at the end of the day is rewarded with a spectacular sunset.

> *Walk back east on Esplanade Elisabeth II for 110 metres, continue onto Avenue de l'Impératrice for 800 metres. Turn right onto Rue Louison Bobet then left after 10 metres. You will see the Hôtel du Palais on the right.*

Hôtel du Palais

As a child Princes Eugénie spent many of her holidays in Biarritz and never forgot the happy times she shared here. When she married Napoleon II she persuaded him to come back with her. Napoleon also fell in love with Biarritz but when it became apparent their chateau was too small for the imperial court he purchased a site overlooking the sea and within six months the Villa Eugénie was built. This villa was eventually known as the Hôtel du Palais.

For sixteen years the couple returned to Biarritz and in time many other famous people came too. The Hôtel du Palais was the perfect place to be. Fire destroyed the hotel in 1903 but it was soon rebuilt and a new wing added. In 1906 King Alfophonse XII of Spain met Princess Ena Battenberg here and they married the following year. Although the visits from royalty dwindled the hotel became popular with many others such as Charlie Chaplain and Ernest Hemmingway. Then when the city was under German occupation the hotel became the home to soldiers.

Hotel du Palais

By the 1950s the hotel had become popular again with its fabulous firework displays and other events. At this time the guestrooms and suites were renovated and a large pool built. Guests such as Bing Crosby, Frank Sinatra, Jane Mansfield and Gary Cooper came as well as the Duke and Duchess of Windsor.

Today if you can afford it you can stay here and enjoy the splendour of a bygone age. If not just pay a visit! With its high ceilings, ornate decorations, chandeliers and marble it is magnificently Belle Époque.

> *Just across the Avenue de l'Impératrice from the Hôtel du Palais you will see the Église Orthodoxe.*

Église Orthodoxe

The connection between Biarritz and Russia goes back to the time when Napoleon III and the Empress Eugénie invited the Russian nobility to spend their summers in Biarritz, helping to mould the town into what it is today.

The Orthodox Church was founded in 1892 after an alliance between France and Russia under the initiative of Tsar Alexander III. It was built in the Byzantine style with an impressive blue dome and icons brought from Saint Petersburg and dedicated to Saint Alexander Neveski.

After the revolution of 1917 the church welcomed the emigrants from Soviet Russia and today people from all nationalities worship here. Over the past 120 years the church has been partially restored but now needs a major restoration.

> *Walk south on Avenue de l'Impératrice for 25 metres, turn left onto Rue de Russie. Turn right after 60 metres onto Rue de l'Université Américaine then left after 85 metres onto Avenue Reine Victoria where you will see the Chapelle Impériale.*

Chapelle Impériale

The Imperial Chapel was built in 1865 on the request of Empress Eugénie and Napoleon III. Designed by the architect Boeswillwald who oversaw its construction it is characterised by a mixture of Romanesque-Byzantine and Hispano-Moorish style and dedicated to Our Lady of Guadalupe the Patroness of Mexico in memory of the war being fought by France.

In 1981 the chapel was classified as an historic monument. Now owned by the city of Biarritz it is open only on Saturdays. Four masses are celebrated here each year, two of which celebrate the deaths of Napoleon and the Imperial Prince.

Walk east on Avenue Reine Victoria for 60 metres, turn right onto Rue Pellot for 100 metres, continue onto Rue de Frias. After 300 metres turn right onto Avenue de Verdun.

Église Orthodoxe

Biarritz – Part 3

> *Turn left after 70 meters onto Rue de l'Abbé Pierre Moussempès. Walk 140 metres, turn right onto Place de la Libération and left to stay on this road. Turn left onto Avenue Charles Floquet, right after 270 metres onto Rue Guy Petit then cross the roundabout. The Musee d'Art Oriental Asiatica will be on the left.*

Musee d'Art Oriental Asiatica

The Asian Oriental Art Museum is located on the edge of the main town but if you are happy to walk there or get a bus it is well worth a visit to experience an introduction to the cultures of Asia. It houses an abundance of ancient Indian, Chinese and Tibetan statues, monuments, ancient paintings, temple artwork and archaeological objects. The museum's permanent collections are divided into individual countries and regions.

The museum was founded between 1997 and 1999 by Michel Postel who left France to found a pharmaceutical company in India. He was passionate about his new country and with his team devoted himself to collecting these objects. It is considered to be the finest collection of its kind outside Paris and has information cards in a number of languages.

> *Walk west on Rue Guy Petit, turn left after 140 metres on Avenue de la Gare. Stay on this road for 60 metres, take the first exit on the roundabout onto Avenue du Maréchal Foch. After 200 metres bear right and you will see the Gare du Midi.*

Gare du Midi

The majestic Art Noveau Midnight Station was erected at the beginning of the twentieth century as the *Gare de la Négresse*, today's present station, had been built away from the town at the request of Empress Eugénie.

The work started in 1906 on the instruction of the architect Adolphe Dervaux. The stone for the monumental front came from Arudy and faces the public garden. Passengers had to take the lift or climb a huge staircase, which is now gone, in order to reach the platforms. Inside there are mosaics by the Maumégean brothers.

Steam trains began arriving at the station in 1911 but when the line was electrified in 1925 the station declined and the last train ran in 1980. After a period of several years when it was unused it was modified so that it could hold shows or conventions with its 1400 seats and stage. Although named *Palais des Festivals* for a while it was eventually given back its original name and became a modern festival centre.

> *The Jardin Publique is just in front of the station.*

Jardin Publique

The public garden was created on the initiative of Henry O'Shea in 1903 to welcome visitors to Biarritz once the Gare du Midi had been opened. Today it is a place to sit and relax although during festival time it becomes a scene of dance.

> *From the public gardens turn right onto Rue Ernest Fourneau then after 75 metres turn left onto Avenue Jaulerry for 80 metres. Continue onto Rue des Halles and the market will be on the right after 60 metres.*

Les Halles Biarritz

The covered market halls were established in 1885 in order to trade milk, poultry and vegetables being brought into Biarritz by donkey. Later the donkeys were replaced by horses and carts. The building then expanded to include a fish market. Adaptions were made in 1949 to replace the side windows with large pieces of glass braced by concrete.

The building has been since upgraded and divided into two buildings. In one you will find the fish market but in the other meat, fruit, vegetables, bread and other Basque specialities. It is well worth a visit and the market is surrounded with shops, cafes and restaurants.

> *Walk west on Rue des Halles for 80 metres then turn right onto Rue Gambetta. Turn right after 30 metres onto Rue Broquedis. The Musée Historique will be on the left after 55 metres.*

Musée Historique de Biarritz

The Biarritz History Museum is located in a former Anglican church and established in 1986. The pretty church of Saint Andrew was built by the British in 1876 but has been transformed into an exhibition space tracing the history of Biarritz.

As well as enjoying the exhibition look at the features of the church itself. The porch is a showpiece, constructed in commemoration of the fallen of France in the Napoleonic Wars. On the right hand side is the family tree of the Bonapartes.

In the chancel are the original doors from the Villa Eugènie, a silk tapestry, a model of the imperial train, a bronze model of the Prince Imperial and other things such as a tea set, books and photographs. In front of the chancel you will find more memorabilia relating to the Imperial family. These include paintings, jewellery, medals, a glove belonging to the prince and a handwritten letter.

> *Walk west on Rue Broquedis for 55 metres, turn right onto Rue Gambetta, continue for 20 metres then turn left onto Rue Alcide Augey. After 150 metres turn right onto Rue Peyroloubilh, turn left after 20 metres onto Rue Mazagran then continue onto Rue du Port-Vieux where the tour began.*
>
> *To see the Côte des Basques and the attractions in this area turn right onto the Esplanade du Port Vieux. Continue walking for 200 metres around the coast onto the Boulevard du Prince de Galles.*

Biarritz – Part 4

Plage de la Côte des Basques

Plage de la Côte des Basques

For the more experienced surfers and those who love the wilder beaches the *Côte des Basques* offers a wonderful view of the Spanish coast and mountains. While the rich frequented *La Grande Plage* the Basques themselves gathered in this area; hence its name. Further along this beach becomes the *Plage Marbella*, again a wild area loved by surfers and bodyboarders. Walking further still you arrive at the large *La Plage Milady,* popular with local residents, young people and wheelchair uses because the beach has been adapted to enable wheelchair users direct access to the sea. Again there are stunning views from the beach.

To visit the Planète Musée du Chocolat or Cité de l'Océan and Côte des Basquesit pick up a number 10 or 13 bus near Les Halles or get the free shuttle from the aquarium. Walking takes 40 minutes.

To walk follow Boulevard de Prince de Galles for 600 metres, turn left on the small road until you come to Avenue Nortre Dame. Turn left, continue for 55 metres, turn right onto Avenue Beau Rivage. Planète Musée du Chocolat is on the right after 120 metres.

Planète Musée du Chocolat

This small museum is worth a visit for anyone interested in the history of chocolate, from when it was first discovered three thousand years ago to the present day. Exhibits include vintage chocolate making equipment, posters and other items. In addition to handmade chocolates there are stunning chocolate sculptures created by a master chocolatier and a tasting session.

> *Walk south on Avenue Beau Rivage for 83 metres. At the roundabout, take the 4th exit onto Place Beau Rivage. After 85 metres continue onto Rue de Madrid for 950 metres, bearing right to stay on this road.*
>
> *Take the 2nd exit at the roundabout onto Avenue de Bidart for 300 metres then turn left onto Avenue de la Plage. Cité de l'Océan will be on the right after 85 metres.*

Cité de l'Océan

The City of the Ocean and Surf was designed by the architect Steven Holl in collaboration with Solange Fabião and opened in 2011. It is part museum, part educational centre and part theme park. The exhibition explores the complex ecosystem of the ocean and what can be done to protect it by looking at its role upon our leisure, science and ecology.

There are many interactive activities for both children and adults that include films, a simulated dive in an underwater bathysphere and an unexpected storm when visiting the wheelhouse of a stranded ship. The museum is a sister site to the aquarium. A free shuttle bus runs between the two.

The Third Tour: Hendaye

Hendaye is a French seaside town on the border with Spain located on the right bank of the River Bidasoa. The river forms a natural border between Spain and France with the town of Hondarribia and the city of Irún just across the water. Its position was an important point for commerce between the two countries but there have been many conflicts between them too.

From the sixteenth to eighteenth centuries the cities of Hendaye, Irún and Hondarribia were continuously at war. In 1793 the old town was completely destroyed by Spanish troops. Tension gradually lessened towards the beginning of the twentieth century and in the Spanish Civil War it became a refuge for many Spanish people escaping from Spain. The old town was eventually rebuilt and became home to the Neo-Basque style of architecture.

Hendaye is roughly divided into three different areas. The old town which lies between the railway station and Saint Vincent's Church that is also partly industrial; the seaside area with its beach and boulevard; the camping sites, château and nature reserve.

Neo-Basque houses on the Bouldevard de Mer

The coming of the railway brought about expansion and Hendaye became popular as a seaside town. The traditional Basque houses can be admired on many streets and those built at the beginning of the twentieth century have been well preserved as part of the town's heritage. The architect Edmond Durandeau was well known for his original and modern constructions in the Neo-Basque style. His aim was to turn Hendaye into one of the leading seaside towns on the Atlantic coast. As well as the buildings on the Boulevard de la Mer his other buildings include the current Bellevue Hotel which can be seen from the Bay Path.

As well as its beautiful buildings Hendaye offers the opportunity to relax on the beach, swim, dive, surf or take part in a range of other nautical activities. Hendaye has a range of festivals that are celebrated throughout the year. There are numerous restaurants in which to enjoy traditional food such as *côte de bœuf a la plancha*, *tapas* or *txurro*, the Basque name for the Spanish *churro* made from dough dusted with cinnamon and sugar.

Hendaye has good transport links. As well as a good train service from other areas of France the local buses offer a regular service within Hendaye and the surrounding towns. Hendaye is served by Hegobus lines 4, 5, 6 and 20. There are also ferries across the river to the town of Hondarribia.

The tour of Hendaye starts at the station and passes through the old town before following the Bay Path with its historical features to the port, marina and beach of the new town. It then explores the wonderful Château d'Abbadia and nature reserve. This last part is a very long walk so you may prefer to take the bus or perhaps split the tour between two days.

Third Tour: Main Sights

- Place de la République
- Église St Vincent
- Fronton Gaztelu Zahar
- Port de Caneta
- Bakar Etchea
- Mémorial de guerre d'Hendaye
- Port de la Floride
- Port de Plaisance
- Sokoburu
- Eskualduna
- Église Sainte-Anne
- Ondarraitz Beach & Les Deux Jumeaux
- Château d'Abbadia
- Domaine d'Abbadia

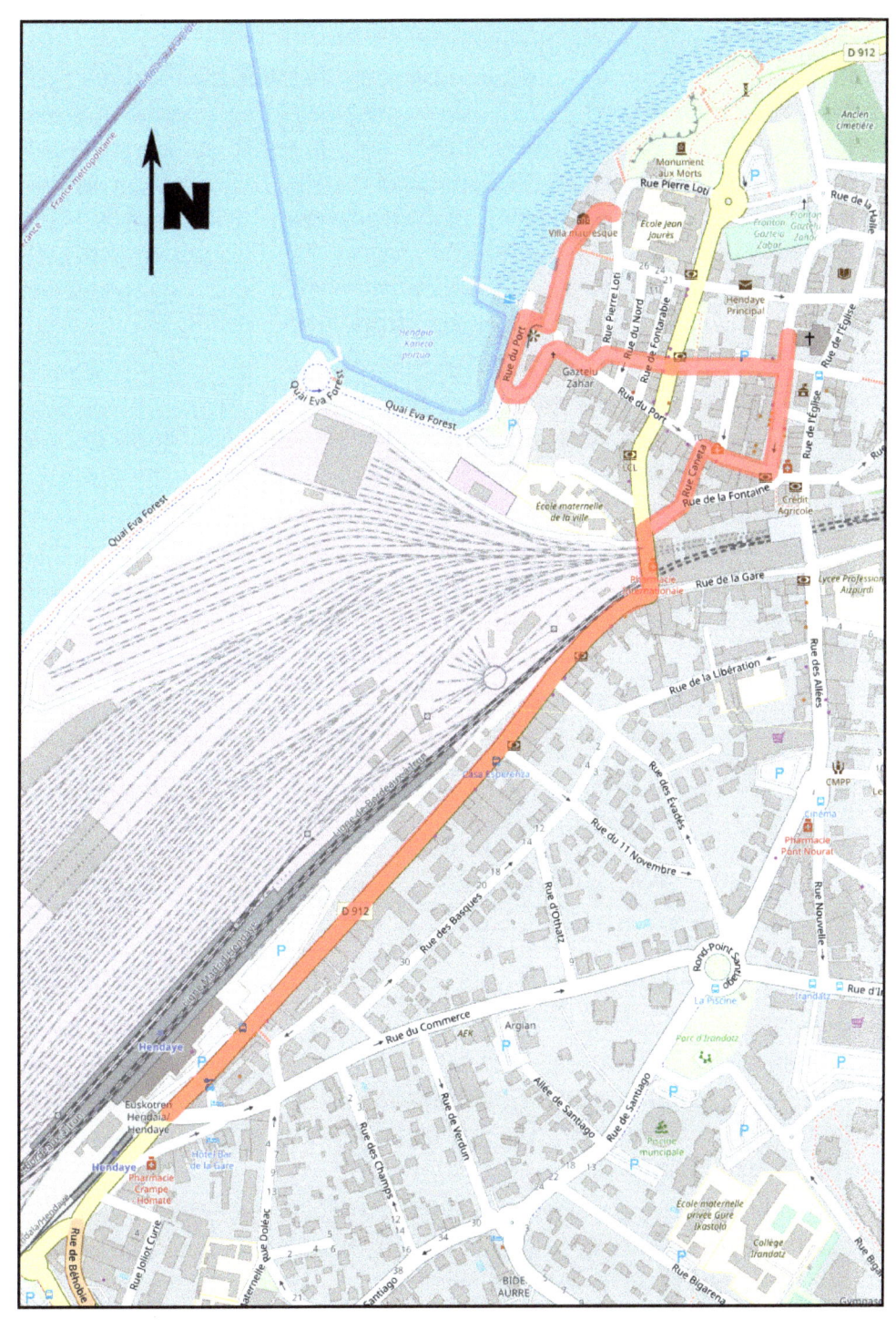

Hendaye – Part 1

Gare d'Hendaye

Hendaye railway station was established on 22nd October 1863 and the first Madrid -Paris train arrived on 15th August 1864 heralding a period of rapid development as Hendaye became a popular seaside resort and international hub being midway between San Sebastián and Biarritz. Hendaye train station serves the Bordeaux to Irún and Madrid to Hendaye lines. It is served by TGV, Intercités long distance, SNFC TER local services, RENFE Arco services and the Euskotren. All trains stop at Hendaye because it is a border station where trains have to change gauge when passing from France into Spain. Between Hendaye and Irún both track gauges run together.

The Euskotren came to Hendaye in 1913. It is the Spanish Basque railway that runs along the coastline from Hendaye to San Sebastián and leaves from a separate station on the forecourt of the main station. It is known locally as *El Topo* which translates as *the mole*.

An historic event took place in an armoured wagon on the tracks of this station at the beginning of World War II. Francisco Franco met with Adolf Hitler to discuss Spain joining the conflict and becoming part of the Axis powers. As Franco's demands were so high no agreement was reached.

The older part of Hendaye is located near to the train station.

> *From the train station walk north-east on Boulevard du Général de Gaulle for 700 metres. Turn right onto Rue Caneta, right after 100 metres onto Rue du Port, then left after 70 metres onto Place de la République.*

Place de la République

Republic Square is the centre of the town and the location of the famous seventeenth century *Great Cross of Hendaye*. The cross is carved with symbols that were said to contain encrypted information about a future global disaster. The information was interpreted as a reminder that a great comet would crash into Earth in the year 2012.

It is thought the cross was constructed in the middle seventeenth century, probably in Germany, before being moved to its present position in the middle of the nineteenth century. It is made up of three parts: a traditional Greek cross, a column and the pedestal base; you will see these parts are subdivided. The cross has three different inscriptions while the base has four symbols.

The square has a number of cafes and terraces where one can sit and enjoy a meal or drink. On Wednesday and Saturday mornings there are two traditional markets held here. Five other markets are also held here on special dates throughout the year.

> *Walk north along Place de la République and continue onto Rue du Vieux Fort. You will see Saint Vincent Church on the right.*

Église St Vincent

Listed as an historic monument the beautifully proportioned Basque Church of Saint Vincent was built in 1598 matching the houses around it with its white walls, exposed stone corners and red shutters. Originally an octagonal bell tower stood on the site. During the wars against Spain the church was destroyed several times between 1793 and 1813. It was enlarged in 1902 and underwent more work in 1968.

The interior has superb decorations that include a crucifix from the thirteenth century, a tabernacle dated 1550, paintings, a golden altarpiece of the Virgin Mary from the sixteenth century and polychrome bas-reliefs from the seventeenth century. Around the nave can be seen the wooden galleries on three levels that are attributed to Jules Maumézean in 1881. As was customary in Basque churches the seating here was reserved for men while the women sat in the room below. The famous French composer Joseph Maurice Ravel was baptised in this church.

> *Walk back south on Rue du Vieux Fort, turn right onto Rue de la Liberté for 170 metres, turn left to stay on this road for 15 metres. Turn right onto Rue du Port and the Pelota building will be on the left.*

Fronton Gaztelu Zahar

The Gaztelu Zahar is a sports hall used for playing the traditional Basque Pelota ball games such as *Cesta Punta* and *Pelota Mano* as well as other events of celebration. It was built in 1899 and named after the fortress built by Vauban that once stood on the same location but was destroyed in the wars between France and Spain.

> *Across the street from the Fronton follow the Rue du Port down to the waterfront to see the Port de Caneta.*

Port de Caneta

Standing on the waterside at the old fishing Port de Caneta, translated from Basque as the *Port of the Pen,* there are wonderful views across of the Bay Txingudi to Hondarribia with the Jaizkibel Mountains. Walking from here along the Rue des Pêcheurs you will get a flavour of the old fishermen's village and cottages.

> *Walk along the waterfront, turn right onto Rue du Port then left after 75 metres onto Rue des Pêcheurs. Follow this road until you meet Rue Pierre Loti. Bakar Etchea is where the two roads meet.*

Bakar Etchea

The last home of Pierre Loti, a French naval office and novelist known for his exotic novels, can be seen on the corner of Rue de Pêcheurs and Rue Pierre Loti. The white walled building with green timbers has a plaque placed upon the upper wall.

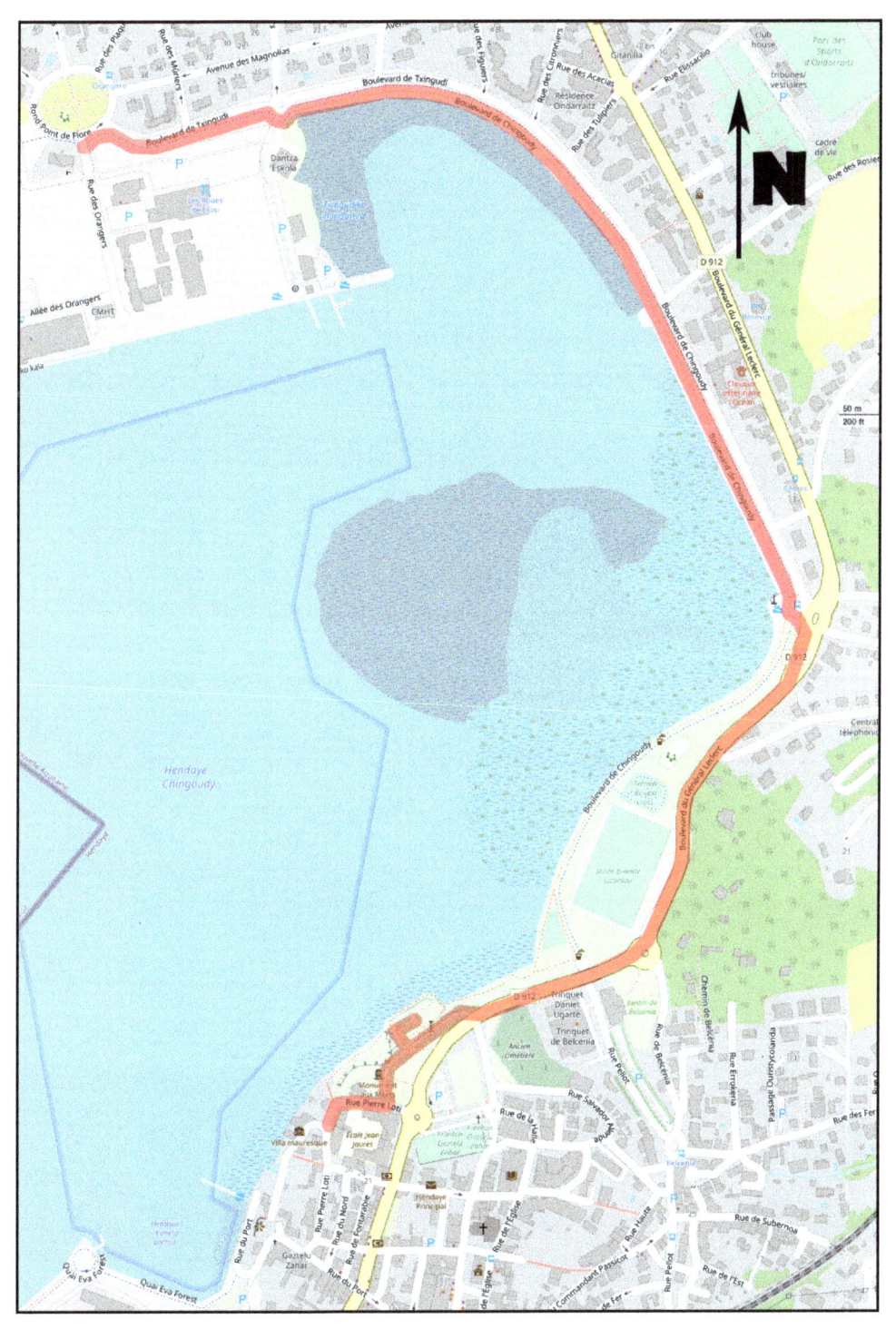

Hendaye – Part 2

> *From the house walk northwards along Rue Pierre Loti for 100 metres then turn left. The War Memorial will be on the left.*

Mémorial de guerre d'Hendaye

The Hendaye war memorial is a monument dedicated to those who lost their lives in the two world wars. Ninety-eight names are inscribed on the monument. On the pilasters framing the monument the areas and battles are inscribed.

In more recent times a stele bearing the Cross of Lorraine was erected at the edge and dedicated to the Escapees of France, the Free French Forces and the Resistance.

In front of the memorial is a bronze sculpture that depicts France holding a dying soldier. A plaster model was first created by Paul Ducuing then it was later cast in bronze by Gustave Leblanc-Barbedienne.

> *From the memorial head back towards the sea and take the Bay Path.*

Hendaye War Memorial and Txingudi Bay

Hendaye Marina

Chemin de la Baie

The Bay Path was the passage for the pilgrims on the road to St Jacques de Compostela. It crossed the bridge that links Hendaye to Irún. Whether you choose to walk or cycle you will be rewarded with panoramic views of the cities of Hondarribia and Irún as you walk around Txingudi Bay.

Walking along the Bay Path you will pass the ruins of the early seventeenth century fortifications that were reinforced by Vauban in 1685 and the old cannons pointing towards Hondarribia. The fort was built in 1618 on the orders of Louis XIII and then enlarged by Vauban on the orders of Louis XIV. It was intended to restore order in the city.

The Spanish people of Hondarribia had prevented anything taking place in this bay and in 1793 the Spanish completely destroyed the fort, the church and most of the town of Hendaye. Today the only part of the fort that remains is next to the war memorial.

Follow the Bay Path until you reach the Port de la Floride and the Quai Floride.

Hendaye – Part 3

Port de la Floride

From the Florida Quay you can again look across the Bay Txingudi. Until 1998 this was just a fishing port with an auction site but since then many nautical enterprises and restaurants have been opened here.

> *Keep walking along the bay and you will arrive at the Port de Plaisance.*

Port de Plaisance

Built in 1990 the Port of Pleasure is the only marina on the Aquitaine coast that is accessible at any time whatever the weather. It is a place of refuge along this coast when the seas are rough. There are a number of restaurants nearby.

From this marina you can enjoy a boat trip, sail, kayak or even jet-ski. This is where you can get the ferry to Hondarribia. It leaves about every fifteen minutes.

> *Walk around the marina until you reach the Avenue des Mimosas then follow the road around until you reach the beach and the Boulevard de Mer.*

Sokoburu

This building is a mixture of Spanish and Basque architecture. Located here is a centre for sea water therapy, a casino, a merchant gallery, a hotel and restaurants.

> *Turn right onto Boulevard de Mer.*

Basque Architecture on Boulevard de Mer

Along the Boulevard de Mer there are about sixty picturesque Neo-Basque properties with different coloured facades. They are known as Neo-Basque because although similar to Basque houses they have a more modern style. Like a traditional farmhouse they have a white façade and wooden half-timbering with asymmetrical roofs and more windows on the outside. Most of them were designed by the architect Edmond Durandeau.

> *Continue walking along Boulevard de Mer until you reach Rue de Eucalyptus. You will see the former Eskualduna hotel.*

Eskualduna

During Hendaye's development as a seaside town many villas with stunning Basque style architecture were built along the Boulevard de Mer in the early twentieth century. The Exkualduna was a former luxury hotel built in the 1910's. In the Roaring Twenties it was the place to be for all the socialites when sea bathing became fashionable. During the two world wars it was used as a rest centre for soldiers then in 1951 converted to a private residence. Take time to walk around the building and view it from all angles.

> *Continue walking along Boulevard de Mer until you come to the roundabout opposite Boulevard du Général Leclerc . The Résidence Croisière is on the left.*

Résidence Croisière

This building of Moorish style architecture was constructed in 1884 and was the symbol of the growth of tourism in Hendaye. From 1889 to 1980 it was the town's casino but was transformed into a private luxury residence and market gallery in 1990. It is also the departure point for the famous GR10 hike from Hendaye to Esterencuby which crosses through the Pyrenees.

Résidence Croisière

> *Continue walking along the Boulevard du Mer. Just after the Rue d'Irún the tourist office will be on the right.*

Office de Tourisme

The Tourist office in Hendaye is the place to pick up a large scale map of the town, information about its attractions with their times of opening and details of local transport. It also has a free Wi-Fi zone. The leaflets available from **www.hendaye-tourisme.fr/en/** include a plan of the town, a guide to the restaurants, suggestions of where to stay and information about sights and activities.

> *Continue walking along Boulevard de la Mer for 200 metres then turn right onto Rue des Prunus until you reach the roundabout. The Church of Saint Anne will be on the right.*

Église Sainte-Anne

The modern church of Saint Anne, the patron saint of sailors and fishermen, stands on the site of an eighteenth century chapel. The church was rebuilt in two sections dated 1924-1927 and 1932-1936 financed by the Countess Paul d'Aramon to plans drawn up by the architects Martinet and Verdeil and blessed in 1937. The fishermen would call at the church to say their prayers before sailing out to sea in search of whales.

The façade has a gable preceded by an open porch. It has a tower at the north-east corner. The original stained glass windows date to 1930 but these have recently been restored by Henri Chaudron, master glassmaker in Béarn.

Inside the apse is surrounded by a walkway which serves three radiating chapels. The organ was built in 1938 by Victor Gonzalez on the instruction of the blind grand organist André Marchal. This is also the subject of a restoration project.

> *Walk back along Rue des Prunus then turn right onto Boulevard de la Mer. From here you can see Ondarraitz Beach and Les Deux Jumeaux.*

Ondarraitz Beach and Les Deux Jumeaux

Walking along Boulevard de la Mer you will have seen the long sandy beach. This three kilometre stretch is known as Ondarraitz Beach and even at its busiest times there is always a relatively secluded spot to sit. The beach is popular with families and surfers. On the Boulevard de la Mer there are a number of shops, bars and restaurants.

If you look towards the far end of the beach you will see the *Les Deux Jumeaux rocks*, translating as *the two bell stones*. Carved out by the action of the waves they have become a symbol of Hendaye. The local legend passed down is that one day a Bigfoot like creature from Basque mythology, known as a *Basajaun*, was in the mountains when he tried to destroy the town of Bayonne by throwing a big rock. As he threw the rock it slipped from his hand then broke into two pieces when it landed on Hendaye beach. There is also a good view of these rocks from Domaine d'Abbadia, a nature park further along the coast.

> *On Boulevard de la Mer it is possible to catch a number 4 or 20 Hegobus to the Château d'Abbadia. Walking takes about half an hour.*
>
> *To walk continue along Boulevard de la Mer which becomes Route de la Cornich/D912 for 1600 metres. Cross over the roundabout, walk 350 metres then turn left for the Château d'Abbadia.*

Château d'Abbadia

The Castle of Abbadia was constructed between 1864 and 1879 to the plans of the architect Viollet le Duc s for the eccentric Antoine d'Abaddie. It is an unconventional Neo-Gothic building inspired by the castles of the Middle Ages with its towers and battlements. The exterior walls of the castle are decorated with numerous stone animal sculptures.

Antoine d'Abaddie was born in Dublin in 1810, the son of an Irish mother and a Basque father. His family was among the two hundred richest families in France. Antoine used his wealth well and made the most of all opportunities that arose. He had many interests that are reflected inside the castle showing his passion for exploration, astrology, geography and culture. He is best known for his work in Ethiopia where he created its first cartographic map and also a dictionary of the Semitic language found there.

Château d'Abbadia

The castle is unique and anyone interested in art or architecture should not fail to visit. It has a central body with three wings. The main staircase is decorated with a beautiful stained glass window depicting the family coat of arms and mottos. You cannot miss the exotic Ethiopian shields and animal horns. Located in the centre of the chateau is the library. When Antoine bequeathed his castle to the Academy of Sciences in 1896 there were more than 10,000 books. The more valuable ones have been transferred to the French National Library in Paris.

The main lounge is circular in shape and located in the South tower with half panelled walls above which the walls are painted in blue. Look out for the gold monograms A for Antoine and V for Virginie in Gothic script. The fireplace is constructed from Angouleme stone and Antoine's coat of arms can be seen on the chimney breast together with his motto.

The bedroom where guests of honour stayed has walls covered in large canvas panels decorated with rosettes and Arabic inscriptions. As well as an inscribed four poster bed there is a fire place decorated with turquoise and yellow majolica tiles engraved with an Arabic proverb.

The chapel with its stained glass windows and the crypt below the altar where Antoine and his wife are laid to rest has red optical illusions on the walls. The rectangular nave could once accommodate the local farmers when they came to worship.

Domaine d'Abbadia

The Field of Abbadia is a protected natural park surrounding the Château d'Abbadia. It is however owned by a different organisation so you have to walk back from the Chateau to one of is entrances. On arrival you will find informative panels and a map to show the trail to follow. The walk along the water with its beautiful views takes around two hours. You will pass the steep grey and pink cliffs, meadows, moors and dense woods. Around thirty species of birds nest here and at the right time of year you will also see rare orchids. In this area there are also some renovated Basque farm houses.

The Fourth Tour: Hondarribia

Hondarribia, known in Spanish as *Fuenterrabía* , is one of the most beautiful towns in the Basque country. It is located at the mouth of the Bidasoa River which forms a natural boundary with Hendaye in France.

There are a number of ways to reach Hondarribia. San Sebastián's airport is located just outside the town and the Ekialdebus Company has buses that connect with both Hondarribia and San Sebastián. However you would need to fly to Barcelona or Madrid before taking a connecting local flight.

Hondarribia doesn't have a bus or train station but there are a number of different bus stops throughout the town that connect with San Sebastián, Irún and other local towns. Trains run to San Sebastián, Irún and Hendaye and it is an easy journey from Hendaye to Hondarribia on the ferry. It costs around €2 and takes just ten minutes.

Due to its position on the Bidasoa River where fords permitted crossing from one country to another Hondarribia became a significant stronghold. The old town protected by it huge walls could only be accessed through two gates: the Puerta de Santa María and the Puerta San Nicolás. The town suffered numerous sieges throughout its history but much of its defensive system can still be viewed today. Walking around the outside of the city walls demonstrates how well the town was fortified while exploring the cobbled streets inside the town gives an understanding of what life was like in mediaeval times.

Hondarribia

Hondarribia was once a fishing village and today is rich in architecture, history and gastronomy. Most of the restaurants and bars for which Hondarribia is famous can be found around the Marina area. In this area too you will see the picturesque Basque houses where the fishermen lived for many centuries that have shutters and wooden balconies painted in a multitude of colours. The different colours were chosen so that fishermen could identify their own houses easily as they came back into port after their fishing trips.

A number of festivals and celebrations take place in Hondarribia. Between the 7th and 11th September is the festival that honours its patron saint the Virgin of Guadalupe. During this time there are Basque dances, Basque sports and children's activities. The biggest celebration is called the *Alarde*. It is a military procession held to celebrate the vows made to the Virgin of Guadalupe in 1639 for breaking the siege imposed by the French troops. The festival comes to an end with a celebration of mass held in memory of all those who died during the siege.

The Festival of Blues is an annual event held since 2006. The Euskal Herria Pintxo Championship is also held to find the best Pintxo making chef.

There is a procession on Good Friday known as the *Procession of Silence*. A medieval market is held on the second Sunday in June while on July 25th the *Feast of the Ark* is celebrated.

The tour begins at the old ferry port pier and explores the marina area where the fishermen lived in their pretty Basque houses. Leaving this neighbourhood it enters the old wall town where you can see the medieval fortifications and wander its cobbled streets before following the waterfront back to the old pier and on to the seaside and fishing port.

Fourth Tour: Main Sights

- Kai Zaharra
- Iglesia de la Marina
- Arrantzaleen Kofradia
- San Pedro Kalea
- Santiago Kalea
- Polborina
- Plaza de Gipuzkoa
- la Puerta de San Nicolás
- San Nikolas Kalea
- Plaza de Armas
- Iglesia de Nuestra Señora del Manzano
- Kalea Nagusia
- Pampinot Kalea
- Apezpicu Plaza/Plaza del Obispo
- Apezpicu Plaza/Plaza del Obispo
- Castillo de San Telmo

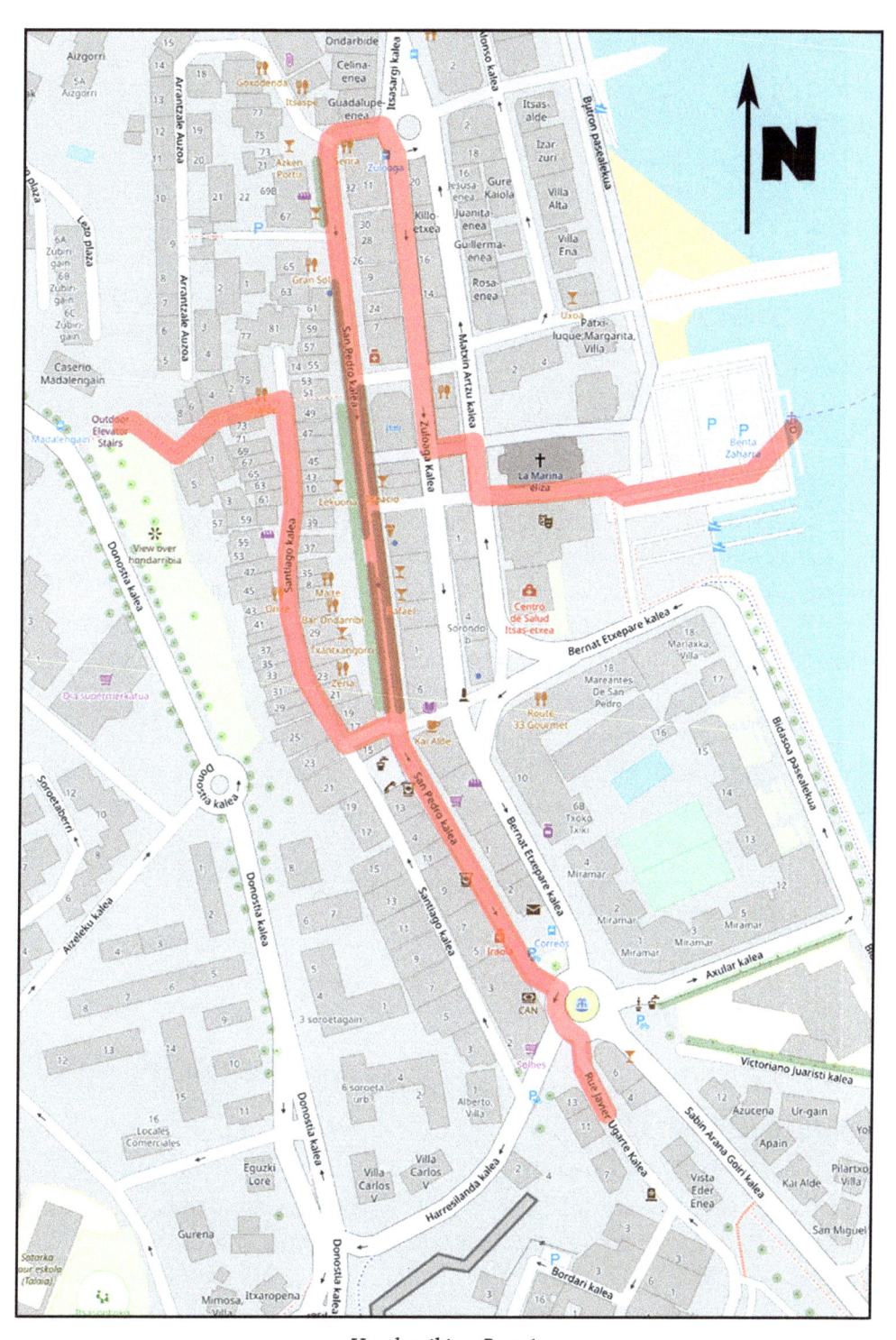

Hondarribia – Part 1

Kai Zaharra

The old pier, known as *Kai Zaharra* in Basque, is where you arrive when you travel on the ferry from Hendaye. From here the town expanded along the beach in both directions. On the old pier there is the Mariñel boat, the last wooden boat of the local fleet.

> *Walk west on Matxin Arzu Kalea for 60 metres. The Iglesia de la Marina will be on the right. Walk onto Matxin Arzu Kalea to see the front of the church.*

Iglesia de la Marina

The Church of the Navy is also known as La Magdalena. It was built in 1921 and named after the old hermitage hospital that existed in the neighbourhood. The old church of Magdalena was believed to be the first church in the city. It was on the route to Santiago de Compostela that the pilgrims walked but destroyed centuries ago during one of the many assaults on the city.

The pretty church is of Gothic style with Renaissance and Baroque editions. It has white walls with exposed stone parts. On the side façade there are arched windows. The bottom of the tower has open arches while the top of the belfry has three arched windows on each side with large round windows between the two. Inside is a fresco painted by Gaspar Montes Iturrioz.

> *Continue along Matxin Arzu Kalea for 40 metres. The Fisherman's Guild is the arched building on the left. Walk through the arch and turn right onto Zuloaga Kalea.*

Arrantzaleen Kofradia

The Fishermen's Guild was established in 1361 to protect the rights of the fishermen and negotiate on their behalf. Its headquarters was the arched building you see in front of you. It was here that the fishermen also stored their nets. Walk through the arch to see both sides of the building and the keystone with the date 1361-1866 engraved upon it. Above the date is a statue of Saint Peter, the patron saint of fishermen.

Today it is home to one of the most famous and traditional restaurants of Hondarribia where Basque food is cooked. Known as La Hermandad de Pescadores it was established in 1947.

> *From the Fisherman's Guild walk north for 120 metres along Zuloaga Kalea to the roundabout. Turn left and left again onto San Pedro Kalea. Walk for 250 metres until you meet Santiago Kalea.*

San Pedro Kalea

San Pedro Street is the main street of the former fishing quarter. It has many cafes, restaurants, bars and shops. Lining the streets are the pretty Basque fishermen's house, painted in an array of colours, reminiscent of the times when the fishermen looked out for their own houses when coming back to shore.

Fishermen's Houses in San Pedro Street

> *Turn right onto Santiago Kalea then right again to stay on this road. Walk for 250 metres until you meet Madalen Karrika Kalea.*

Santiago Kalea

Santiago is the oldest part of the marina area. Like San Pedro Street it is full of the colourful fishermen's houses with their painted timbers and balconies.

> *Turn right onto Madalen Karrika Kalea. At the end of alley use the escalator for a superb view of the town and harbour before retracing steps to turn right onto Santiago Kalea.*
>
> *Walk for 150 metres, left for 25 metres then right onto San Pedro Kalea. Continue for 140 metres until San Kristobal Plaza. Take the 2nd exit from roundabout onto Javier Ugarte Kalea. The Polborina will be on the right after 45 metres.*

Santiago Kalea, Hondarribia

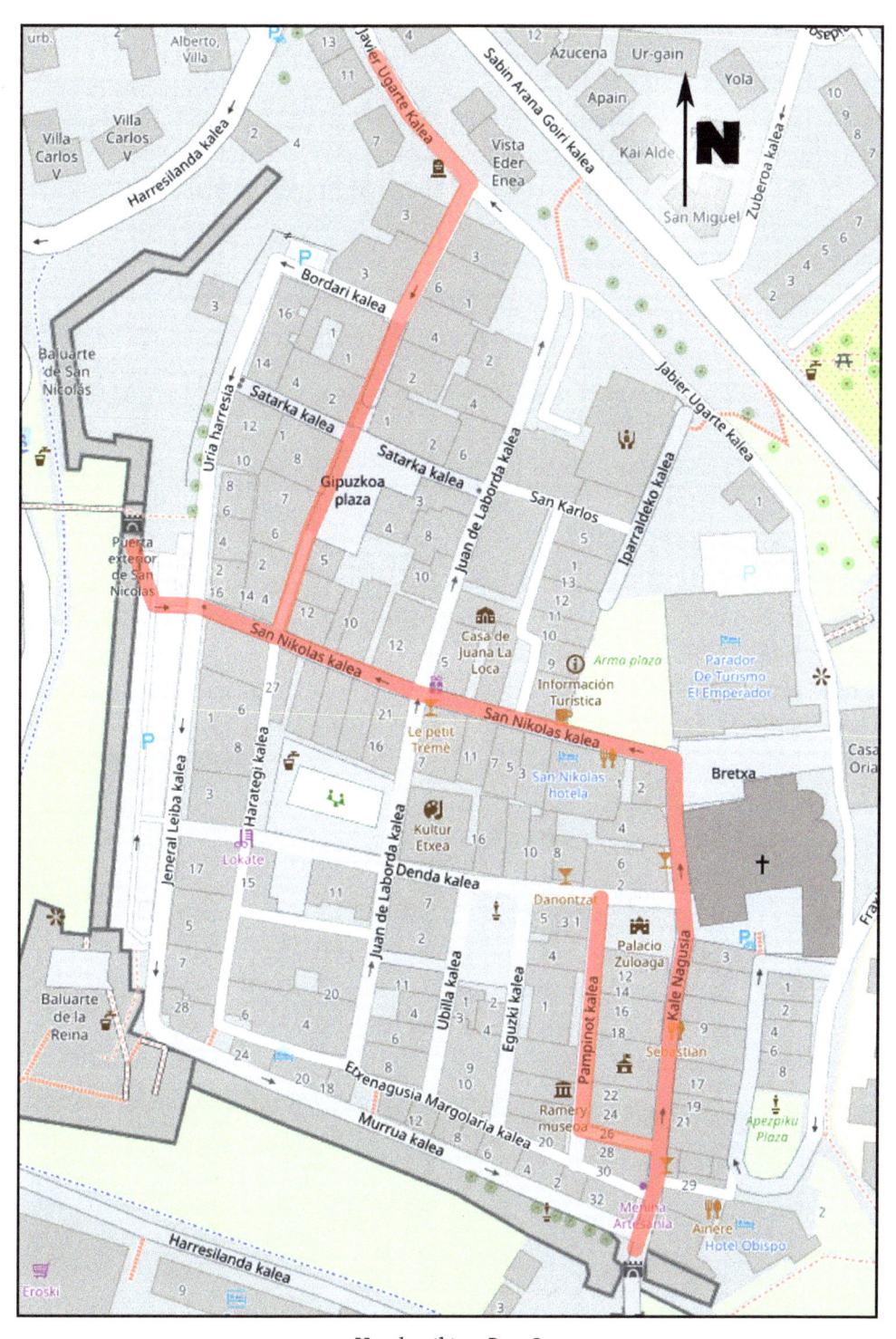

Hondarribia – Part 2

Polborina

The Polborina is a seventeenth century gunpowder store with a stonework vault. The building has been well preserved and can be visited by arrangement with the tourist office in Plaza de Armas. Today a fantastic audio-visual presentation has been integrated into the building to explain its purpose and other information about the old city. It is known as the Amurallda City Interpretation Centre.

> *Continue walking for 65 metres then turn right onto Santiago Konpostela Kalea, walk 90 metres straight on for Gipuzkoa Plaza.*

Plaza de Gipuzkoa

Leaving Santiago Konpostela Kalea you enter the square through a Jacobean Gate. The Gipuzkoa Square is one of the most picturesque in the old town. Although it was constructed in the twentieth century it is a wonderful example of how new constructions can be integrated into a medieval layout such as Hondarribia. It is the work of Architect Manuel Manzano Monis.

Plaza de Gipuzkoa

The small square has a haunting atmosphere of past times with its colourful stone and timber Basque houses and paved floor. There are art galleries located here and a number of cultural events are held in the square.

From the Plaza continue onto Harategi Kalea for 36 metres until you meet San Kikolas Street. Turn right and follow the road round to see La Puerta de San Nicolás.

La Puerta de San Nicolás and San Nikolas Kalea

Saint Nicholas Street is a small cobbled street with colourful narrow tall houses, many with timbered or iron balconies. Look up and compare the simple or double eaves.

At the end of Saint Nicholas Street are the remains of the Gate of Saint Nicholas. There are two gates, one a simple arch belonging to the medieval section of the town and the most recent one dating to the sixteenth century. This had a part permanent bridge and part drawbridge which straddled the moat. Today the footbridge has been restored and provides an ideal way to enter from the town. From here you can see the sixteenth century bastion which is one of the preserved of its kind with its underground passageways.

Walk along San Nikolas Kalea for 120 metres. Turn left into Harma Plaza.

Plaza de Armas

Harma Plaza or Plaza de Armas translates as Weapons Square which for centuries has been the main square of Hondarribia. It was originally the parade ground of the garrisons stationed here but since then bullfights, receptions, proclamations and many other celebrations have been held here. Today there are a number of bars and restaurants in the square.

Plaza de Armas

Visit the tourist office in the Arma Plaza building for a map and other information such as the cultural activities and main tourist attractions. There is a permanent exhibition on the first floor devoted to the town's history and heritage while other temporary exhibitions are housed on the top floor.

Two sides of the square are filled with typical Basque houses while the third offers a view of the Bidasoa estuary in Txingudi Bay. On the fourth side of the square is the Castle of Carlos V which in 1968 became the Parador Hotel.

The original castle was built by Sancho Abarca of Navarre but fortified and expanded by King Sancho II of Pamplona in 1190. It is known today as the Castle of Carlos V due to the extension and restoration he carried out in the sixteenth century. The austere building was both a castle and a palace with six floors for the troops, warehouses, ammunition depot and gunpowder, dungeons and stables.

The castle on the hill overlooking the river, bay and town of Hendaye was perfectly located for defence, hence the garrison being billeted here. Over the years many important people have stayed. In 1660 the Spanish Royal family spent time in the palace while waiting for the marriage of the Infant Maria Teresa to Louis XIV. This marriage, together with the *Treaty of the Pyrenees* signed on Pheasant Island ended the long conflict between Spain and France.

The building was seriously damaged by French troops at the end of the eighteenth century and was a ruin until its transformation into the Parador Hotel. Even if you are not staying at the hotel pay a visit to the hotel bar at the side entrance to see the inside.

> Walk from Plaza de Armas onto Nagusi Kalea to view the church.

Iglesia de Nuestra Señora del Manzano

The Church of Saint María and the Apple Tree is built on the ruins of the old walls replacing a previous Romanesque church. The construction, between the fifteenth and sixteenth centuries lasted so long because of conflicts at the time. Material intended for the construction of the church was used instead for the fortifications. The building was eventually consecrated in 1549.

The church is mainly build in Gothic style but some Renaissance style elements were added later. It has a Latin cross floor plan with three naves. The main entrance built in 1566 opens onto the main street. The oldest part of the church is the side that faces the castle with its large ogee arched entrance. On the left is the town's original coat of arms. Four large windows were added at the beginning of the twentieth century. The church has an eighteenth century Baroque bell tower built by the architect Francisco de Ibero.

Inside there is a starred vault underneath the choir and a decorated segmental arch adorned with religious and heraldic imagery. The beautiful organ should not be missed. The wooden Renaissance altarpiece has been replace by a new Neo-Classical one but fragments of previous altarpieces are preserved in the sacristy. Here also are a number of delicate garments thought to have been used at the wedding of Princess Maria Theresa and King Louis XIV.

> Continue south along Kalea Nagusia to see other points of interest.

Kalea Nagusia

Kalea Nagusia is the main street in the old town. As this was the most important street in the old city the Nobles built their ostentatious houses and palaces here to attract important new friends.

In this cobbled street you can appreciate the fine architecture of the buildings with their wrought iron balconies and family crests. Look up to see the carved beams under the eaves.

House number 4 is unique with its façade of vitrified blue brick. It was built in the seventeenth century and known *as Ladrón de Guevara,* the Thief of Guevara.

House number 5 is the Baroque Casadevante Palace which was restored to become the Hotel Pampinot. It comprises a ground floor and two upper floors, each with moulded openings. On the first floor these openings are topped by pediments decorated with pyramids and balls with the house shield being located in the middle. It was here that the terms of the truce of the Siege of 1638 were negotiated.

The eighteenth century Palacio Zuloaga is house number 8, the home of the Count of Torre-Alta. It was built in 1753 by Pedro Ignacio de Zuloaga and Moyua on the ruins of a palace destroyed on the site of 1638. The main façade facing the street is of ashlar masonry with bays profusely decorated by the use of baroque split pediments. Today the Historical Archive and Municipal Library are located here. You can go inside to look at the interior.

The Baroque Casa Consistorial is house number 20 and today the Town Hall. It is an ornate building constructed from sandstone with a ground floor, mezzanine and noble floor. The ground floor has a porch with three arches while the three bays of the main façade are separated by two large city shields and a balcony. Look out for the carved wooden dogs on the pronounced eaves.

From the Town Hall continue south for 40 metres then turn right onto Etxenagusia Margolari Kalea. Walk 40 metres before turning right onto Pampinot Kalea.

Pampinot Kalea

Pampinot Street has a Gascon name and is home to the seventeenth century Casa Rameri. All the houses in the street are of historic importance but Rameri House, which is number 16, has a spectacular façade decorated with images, mouldings and rosettes. Today the house is home to the head offices of the Francisco de Ibero Institute.

In this street you will find the *Frantzes Putzua* , a sixteenth century French well that was vital to the city during the many sieges that took place. There were many public and private wells in the city. This one is 15 metres deep and always contains water, even in times of drought.

> *Retrace steps back to Etxenagusia Margolari Kalea, walk for 30 metres and turn right onto Nagusi Kalea. The Puerta de Santa María is is at the end of the street.*

Houses Within the Walled City of Hondarribia

Puerta de Santa María

The Door of Saint Mary was once the main entrance to the old town. Originally three gateways were located here but only the middle one survives today as the other two were destroyed by the French army in 1795. It originally had a drawbridge, garrison and a chapel.

Above the arch is the City coat of arms dated 1694. The sixteenth century cube of Santa María can be seen on the left. From here it is possible to see the medieval city walls.

Puerta de Santa Maria

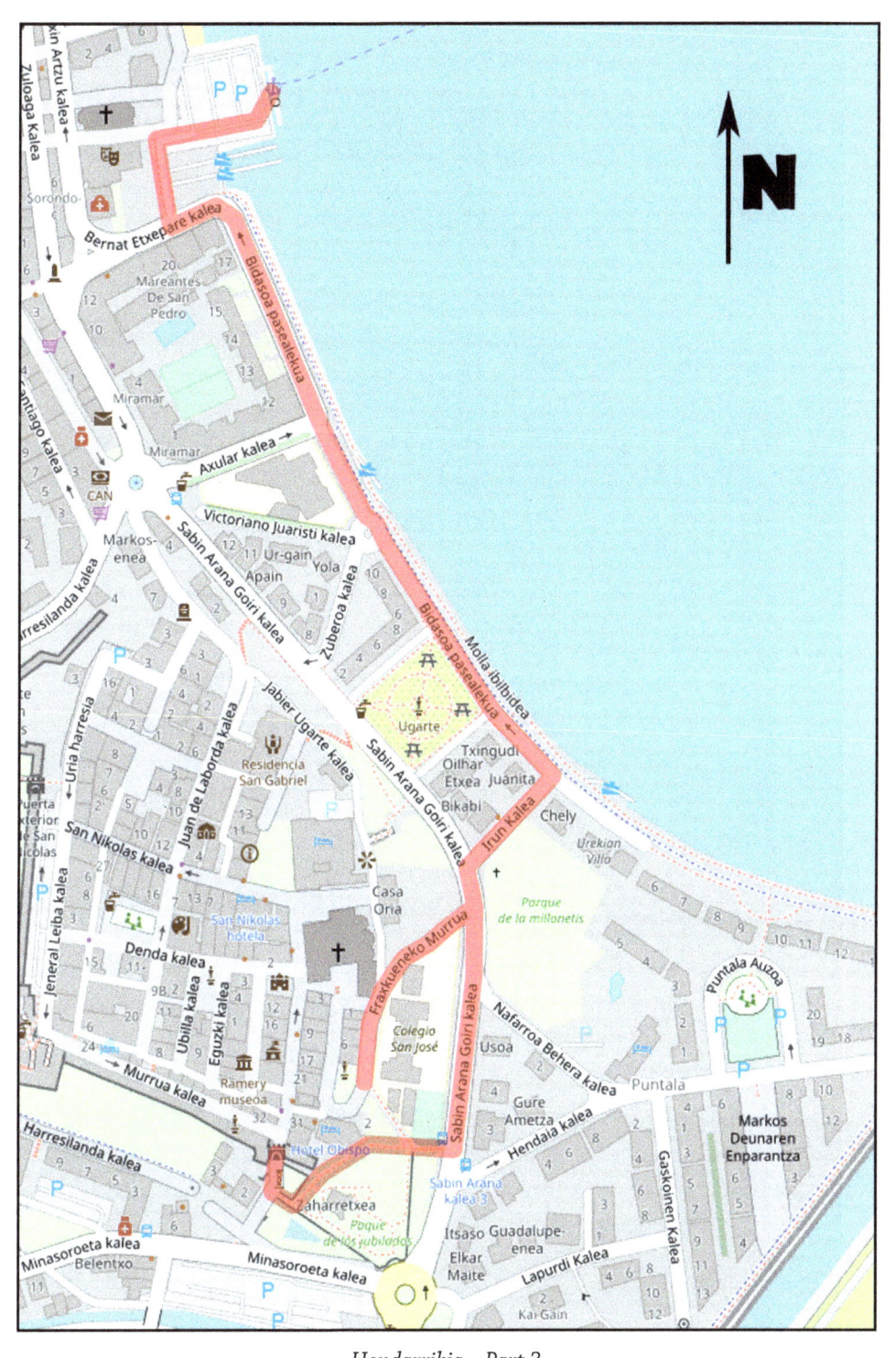

Hondarribia – Part 3

> *Walk south for 15 metres, turn left, walk 130 metres to Sabin Arana Goiri Kalea. Continue for 160 metres, turn right on Irún Kalea. Walk 85 metres to Bidasoa Ibilbidea then turn left onto Fraxkueneko Murrua Kalea. Follow the road round to Bishop's Square.*

Apezpicu Plaza/Plaza del Obispo

Bishop's Street, known as *Apezpicu Kalea* or *Calle del Obispo* is one of the oldest streets in Hondarribia and known by its current name since the sixteenth century. Here Don Cristóbal de Rojas y Sandoval, the future Archbishop of Seville, chaplain to King Charles V and protector of Saint Theresa was born. The statue of this eminent man stands in front of his family home, the *Casa Palencia* or *Echevestenea* in the square that bears his name. His home is now the Hotel del Obispo.

> *Walk back to Sabin Arana Goiri Kaleaand, turn left then right onto Irún Kalea, continue for 85 metres. Turn left onto Bidasoa Ibilbidea. Follow this road back to the ferry port.*
>
> *The beach, marina and fishing port can be reached by following the coastal path for about 25 minutes. A further walk of 900 metres will bring you to Castillo de San Telmo. The Bus E25 goes along coast.*

Playa de Hondarribia

The beautiful beach of Hondarribia is 800 metres long and flanked by a superb promenade that continues along to the fishing port. The waters are calm and it is a popular spot for families, especially with children. There are lifeguards and facilities such as toilets, showers and changing rooms.

Hondarribia has one of the most important and iconic fishing fleets along the Basque coast with the local fishermen engaging in sustainable traditional fishing methods.

Walk on along the coast road from the fishing port for 150 metres. On the bend of the road you can see San Telmo Castle.

Castillo de San Telmo

Saint Telmo castle is also known as *Pirates Castle* as it was built to keep the boats in the harbour of Asturiaga below safe by looking out for pirates and raiders. This harbour was used as a port in Roman times. The castle was commissioned by Don Juan Velázquez, Captain of Gipuzkoa, in 1598 and designed by the engineer Felipe Cramer.

Made in sandstone masonry the north and east sides face the sea with a battery for five guns on the terrace. The segmental arch, guarded by a superb garitón gives access from the front.

View of Town and Port from Top of Escalator

The Fifth Tour: San Sebastián

The town of San Sebastián, known in Basque as *Donostia*, is a Spanish coastal city located on the shores of the Cantabrian Sea in the Bay of Biscay. It is famous for its white sandy beaches, architecture, food and cultural events.

San Sebastián has a small airport located 20 kilometres away just outside the town of Hondarribia. The airport offers direct flights to Madrid and Barcelona. The bus from the airport arrives in Gipuzkoa Square and takes 30 minutes. Biarritz airport is 50 kilometres away with good train and bus connections. Bilbao airport is 100 kilometres away but there is a bus every hour to the city.

The main bus station is located in Plaza Pio XII in the Amara neighbourhood. Here you will also find the Basque railway network known as the *Euskotren* which runs along the coast to Hendaye. The main railway station is located at Paseo de Francia 22 and is known as *Estación de Atocha* or *Estación del Norte*. From here you can take trains to other parts of Spain, France and Portugal. The overnight trains to Paris and Lisbon also leave from here.

The town has three beautiful beaches that are wonderful for sunbathing, swimming and surfing. Along the promenade of La Concha beach, lined with ornate white railings and described as the most beautiful city beach in Europe you will see opulent mansions and other points of interest. The hilltops of Mount Urgull and Mount Igueldo provide stunning views over the city.

San Sebastián has an amazing array of festivals and cultural events that still bring the rich and famous to the city. These include the International Film Festival, Music Festivals, Gastronomic Festivals and events celebrating Basque culture held in the large public squares, the Teatro Victoria Eugenia, the Tabakalera or in the Kursaal. The *Tamborrada,* also known as San Sebastián Day, is the city's most important festival and celebrated in January.

San Sebastián has a reputation for being a great place for food with its renowned restaurants and Tapas Bars, especially in the Old Town which has the highest concentration of bars in the world. Enjoy eating fresh oysters accompanied by the light sparkling wine known as *txakoli* or choose a selection of Basque Tapas known as *Pintxos*. Walking the narrow streets of the Old Town and relaxing in one of the bars is a must on a visit to this city.

The newer part of the town, often referred to as the *Romantic Centre* has a charm of its own. Made famous as a destination for Spanish Royalty and other aristocrats the streets are lined with elegant buildings, ornate bridges, plazas and parks of the Belle Époque era.

The tour begins on the María Cristina Bridge just across from the main railway station. It explores different areas of the town and its beaches before finishing with a funicular ride up Mount Igueldo. It is a very long tour and could be split over two days. Some parts like the climb up Mount Urgull are long and challenging.

If you want to shorten the tour by missing out this part take a shorter route from the Basilica of Saint Mary by walking south-west on 31 de Agosto then taking the stairs onto Kanpandegi Kalea before turning left onto Ijentea Kalea for the City Hall and Park. You can then resume the tour from this point.

Fifth Tour: Main Sights

- Puente María Cristina
- Catedral del Buen Pastor de San Sebastián
- Puente Santa Catalina
- Playa de Zurriola
- Kursaa and Puente Del Kursaal
- De Okendo Plaza
- Parte Vieja and the Plaza de la Constitución
- Iglesia de San Vicente
- Musée San Telmo
- Iglesia de Santa Maria del Coro
- Mont Urgull and Castillo de La Mota
- Paseo Nuevo and the Construcción Vacía
- El Aquarium de San Sebastián
- Museo Naval
- Alderdi Eder Parkea and Ayuntamiento de San Sebastián
- Playa de La Concha and La Perla
- Palacio de Mirimar and Jardines de Miramar
- Playa de Ondarreta and Estatua de María Cristina
- Ferrocarril funicular
- Monte Igueldo

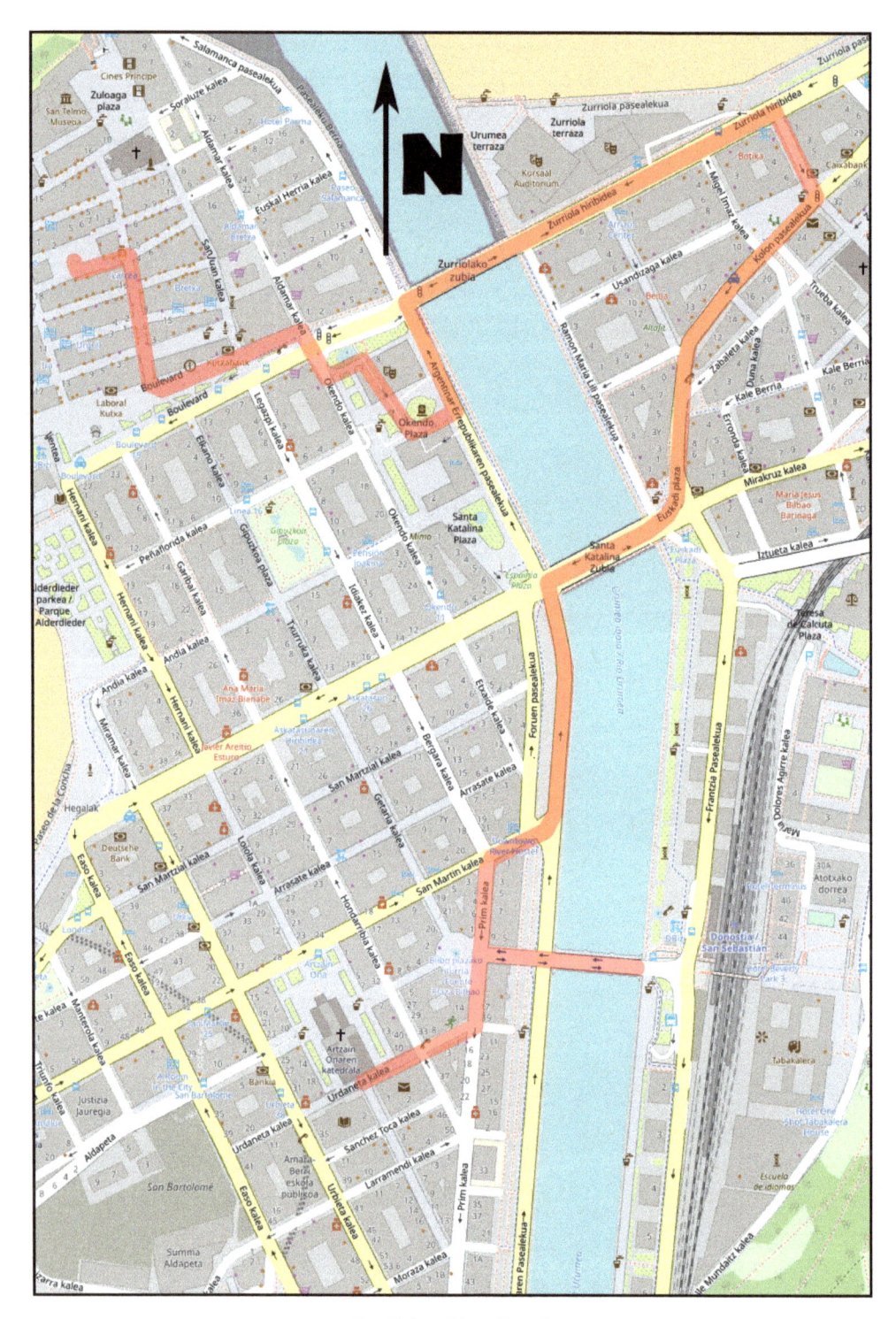

San Sebastián – Part 1

Puente María Cristina

Puente María Cristina

The María Cristina Bridge is the most beautiful bridge in San Sebastián. It crosses the River Urumea linking the city centre with the Estación del Norte, the main railway station. In 1893 a temporary wooden footbridge had been built across the river.

It was designed by the engineer José Eugenio Ribera and the architect Julio María Zapata. Built in the year 1904 in a record nine months it has three spans and mimics the Alexander III Bridge in Paris, with its four obelisks at the ends marking the entrances and the sculptural groups that crown them. On each obelisk are three polychrome shields. The equestrian figures crowning the obelisks were made by the sculptor from Madrid, Ángel García Díaz.

The bridge is constructed from reinforced concrete but the red coverings and decoration are made from artificial stone. It was named in honour of the queen consort of Spain María Cristina de Habsburgo-Lorraine who spent the summer in the city.

Cross the Maria Cristina Bridge and continue onto Valentin Olano Kalea. Turn left onto Prim Kalea, turn right after 65 metres onto Urdaneta Kalea. The Cathedral will be on the right after 130 metres.

Catedral del Buen Pastor de San Sebastián

The Cathedral of the Good Shepherd of San Sebastián sits in the *Buen Pastor Plaza,* the Good Pastor Square which dates from the twentieth century. As well as the Cathedral other buildings such as the Correos Post Office and Koldo Mitxelena Culture Centre can be seen here.

San Sebastián Cathedral was built by the architect Manuel de Echave. With its ogival arch it is similar to the medieval churches in France and Germany. Although work began in 1888 and was delayed due to a lack of resources it still only took nine years to build and was completed in 1897.

The Royal Family were invited to lay the foundation stone. The sandstone used to build the Neo-Gothic cathedral came from Mount Igueldo. The vaults were made with tufa from Alava and the slates for the roofs brought from Angers in France.

Built on a Latin cross design it has three naves. These are segmented into five rectangular sections covered with four part vaults of simple ribbing. The building has been restored and modernised twice. The ceiling and stained glass windows were changed and the wooden floor replaced with the current elegant marble one.

On the main façade is the *Cross of Peace*, the work of sculptor Eduardo Chillida. There are two large rose windows. The slender bell tower inspired by the spires of Cologne Cathedral is 75 metres high and at present is the tallest building in San Sebastián.

Inside you can still see the sculpture of the Good Shepherd that stood on the original Neo-Gothic altar and the figures of the four evangelists. Both sculptures were created by the Barcelonan artist Joseph Llimona. Other interesting items are the altars and shrines of the Holy Family, Saint Francis of Assisi, Our Lady of Mount Carmel, Teresea of Ávila and Our Lady of Perpetual Help; all the work of Julio Gargallo.

The stained glass window designed by Juan Bautista Lázaro was made by the workshop of Bolinaga and Cía from León, and Pujol from Barcelona. The seven double windows of the apse depict the twelve apostles and the Sacred Hearts of Jesus and Mary.

The organ that replaced a previous one was installed in 1954 and was said to be the largest one in Spain. It comprises five keyboards for hands, one for feet and 106 stops; in the presbytery is an *echo organ* with two manual keyboards, pedals and 20 stops. The choir organ has 9,535 pipes. The largest pipe measures 10 meters.

> *Walk back 130 metres along Urdaneta Kalea, turn left onto Prim Kalea, walk 160 metres, turn right onto San Martin Kalea; continue for 60 metres. Turn left onto Foru Pasealekua, after 230 metres turn right onto Puente de Santa Catalina*

Puente Santa Catalina

The bridge of Saint Katherine was the first to be built in San Sebastián. It was originally a wooden bridge built in the fourteenth century but was destroyed and rebuilt a number of times due to its strategic position. Until the nineteenth century it was the only bridge linking both banks of the river.

The current Neo-Classical bridge was designed by the architect Antonio Cortázar. The bridge has four arches and is constructed from ashlar masonry with light-coloured stones from Mutriku and red limestones from Ereño. The iconic lampposts installed in 1926 are attributed to Juan Alday.

Stand on the bridge for a wonderful view of the river, other bridges across the river and the buildings of San Sebastián. You can walk to the next attraction along the river bank but the slightly quicker route through the town gives a flavour of some of the modern buildings.

> *Cross the bridge and walk north-east across the plaza onto Kolon Pasealekua for 400 metres. Turn left onto Ramon y Cajal Kalea for 100 metres and the Playa de Zurriola is ahead.*

Playa de Zurriola

Zurriola beach is popular with the locals and young who like to surf here and practice other water sports. The waves are bigger as it is not in a protected bay like the other beaches in San Sebastián. Several major championships are held here throughout the year. Although perfect for sunbathing parts are more hazardous for swimming due to the undercurrents. There are lifeguards, dressing rooms and showers along with bars and cafes nearby.

The beach is 800 metres long and has views of Mont Ulía. The wall known as *El Muro* at the far eastern end of the beach is a popular place to sit while watching the surfers or enjoying the sunset over the beach.

> *Walk south-west on Zurriola Hiribidea for 150 metres. The Kursaal will be on the right.*

Kursaal

The Kursaal is a congress centre with a large auditorium and many exhibition halls. The original building was an elegant palace built in 1921 that had a cinema, restaurant, casino and other rooms but it was demolished in 1973.

The present building was designed by the Spanish architect Rafael Moneo and opened in 1999. It is home to the largest film festival in Spain known as the *San Sebastián International Film Festival*. It is quite spectacular when lit at night, especially if you are lucky enough to see the rainbow flag colours.

> *Walk from the Kursaal onto the Puente Del Kursaal.*

Puente Del Kursaal

The Kursaal Bridge is also known as the Zurriola Bridge. It was built in 1921 and is the closest bridge to the mouth of the Urumea River. The lampposts here are a must to view. The white and black columns are topped with globes, designed by Victor Arana in the Art Deco style of the time.

> *Cross the bridge, turn left onto República Argentina Kalea. You will see the De Okendo Plaza gardens, Victoria Eugenia Theatre and María Cristina Hotel on the right.*

Puente Del Kursaal

De Okendo Plaza

The beautiful square planted with palm trees and flower beds takes its name from Admiral Antonio Okendo who was a military man in the San Sebastián Navy. His statue stands in the square.

The theatre of Victoria Eugenia located here was inaugurated in 1912 but was renovated and reopened in 2007. With its Belle Époque style it is one of the most symbolic buildings in San Sebastián.

The hotel in was designed by the architect Charles Mewes who was responsible for the Ritz hotels in Paris and Madrid. The Maria Cristina hotel was opened in 1912 when the regent Maria Cristina became the first visitor. The hotel soon became a favourite place to stay for the aristocrats and royals who came to visit the city.

With the famous film festival held in the town since 1953 the hotel attracted stars such as Elizabeth Taylor, Bette Davis, Woody Allen, Julia Roberts, Richard Gere and Brad Pitt.

> *Walk north-west along the back of the De Okendo Plaza until you reach Boulevard Zumardia. Turn left for 70 metres then cross to the other side of the road. The tourist office will be on the right after 50 metres.*

San Sebastián Tourist Information Centre

At the tourist office you can pick up a large map of the city and information about its sights. The tourist office also keeps City Cards for multiple public transport journeys or sells boat trip tickets.

> *Walk west along Boulevard Zumardia for 35 metres. Turn right onto Narrika Kalea for 130 metres, left onto Arrandegi Kalea for 30 metres then right onto Plaza de la Constitución.*

Parte Vieja and the Plaza de la Constitución

Constitution Square is the centre of the old town known as *Parte Vieja*. It is the main square in the city and the location for many of the celebrations that take place. The square was originally the bullfighting arena. If you look above the windows in each of the houses you will see a number that once marked the bullring boxes.

The Neo-Classical square was established in 1817 under the plans of the architect Ugartemendia who was responsible for rebuilding much of San Sebastián after the siege and disastrous fire of 1813. Today it is home to shops, restaurants and bars. San Sebastián's City Hall was located here until the 1940s.

Plaza de la Constitución

San Sebastián – Part 2

> *Walk to the north-east corner of the plaza, take Iñigo Kalea then turn left after 30 metres onto Narrika Kalea. Walk 40 metres, turn right onto San Vicente Kalea, left after 65 metres onto San Juan Kalea. The church of Saint Vincent will be on the left. Walk all around the church onto Agosto Kalea.*

Iglesia de San Vicente

Built in the first half of the sixteenth century the striking Gothic church of Saint Vincent is said to be the oldest monument in the city. The original church was thought to have been Romanesque and built at the end of the seventh century.

The master stonecutters Miguel de Santa Celay and Juan de Urrutia designed and oversaw the present church's construction. It was one of the few buildings that survived the fires when Napoleon torched the city in 1813.

The church has a rectangular floor plan with three naves, the central one being the tallest. There is a transept aligned with the side naves and an octagonal apse. The ribbed vaults are supported by circular small columned pillars on the inside and by flying buttresses on the exterior.

In the nineteenth century the towers by Echeveste were added and also a semi-octagonal baptistry. The ornate rose windows endowed by the Duke of Mandas were installed in 1923. The stained glass is quite impressive. The Baroque portico is attributed to Domingo Zaldua.

Look out for the sculpture of the *Pieta* on the façade of the church hung in 1999. The sculpture is based on Jorge Oteiza's sketches for the frieze in the Sanctuary of Arantzaz and made by the sculptor José Ramón Anda under the close supervision of Oteiza himself.

One of the finest Romanesque altarpieces, the work of Ambrosio de Bengoechea and Juan de Iriarte can be seen inside. It comprises a pedestal with several panels portraying scenes of Christ's suffering and death. The French organ dating from 1868 is by Cavaille-Coll.

> *Walk across Zuloga Plaza for the entrance to San Telmo Museum*

Musée San Telmo

The first San Telmo museum was built in 1900 on a tight budget so the city mayor, José Machinbarrena, asked local people to donate objects and money. In time the building became much too small and so it moved, only to find once again there was not enough space for the exhibits.

It was then decided to convert the sixteenth century Dominican monastery of San Telmo into the present museum in 1932. The museum has been restored and updated and is divided into two buildings. The older convent building has a unique architecture with its mixture of Gothic and Renaissance styles. The new one designed by the architects Nieto and Sobejano is contemporary and cutting-edge adding to the complex by creating a blend of old and new.

The museum has a number of permanent exhibitions as well temporary exhibits which vary over a period of time. There are over 26,000 exhibits dedicated to Basque culture and history enabling a deeper insight into Basque society.

> *Walk south-west on Santa Korda Kalea for 64 metres, turn left onto De Valle Lersundi Plazatxoa, right after 35 metres onto 31 de Agosto Kalea/Abuztuaren 31 Kalea then continue for 120 metres. The Basilica of Saint Mary will be on the right.*

Iglesia de Santa Maria del Coro

The ostentatious church of Saint Mary of the Chorus is one of the most important churches in the city. It is a Baroque Roman Catholic church and was completed in 1774. Long before this time another church stood here attached to the fortified city walls.

The present church was designed by Pedro Ignacio de Lizardi although he was influenced by Miguel de Salezán and Domingo de Yarza. It stands at an angle between Kalea Nagusia and Agosto Kalea. The ornate main entrance sits between two towers and has a figure of Saint Sebastián carved above it. The city shield crowns the building. The main door runs in a straight line to the entrance of Buen Pastor Cathedral.

Iglesia de Santa Maria del Coro

The main nave is divided into three which then becomes subdivided into four parts. At the end of the nave are the daily chapel and the sacristy. Six pillars act as buttresses to support the vaults. The central dome is 27 metres high. The altarpiece is dedicated to Saint Maria, the city's patron saint. Next to the baptismal font is a cross-shaped sculpture by Eduardo Chillida.

> Walk south-west on 31 de Agosto Kalea/Abuztuaren 31 Kalea/San Telmo Kalea towards Calle Mayor/Kale Nagusia, continuing to stay on Agosto Kalea for 230 metres.
>
> Take the stairs, bear left onto Monte Urgull Kalea for 160 metres then left onto Gaztelubide Kalea for 350 metres. Turn right to stay on Gaztelubide Kalea. The Castillo de la Mota will be on the right after 160 metres.

Mont Urgull and Castillo de La Mota

Although it's quite a hike up to the top of Mount Urgull it is a splendid thing to do. The views from the top with the Sacred Heart Statue presiding over the summit are stunning. There are unique views of the city and sea from scenic lookout points along the way.

The Castillo de la Mota fortress stands at the highest point on Mount Urgull. It was built in the twelfth century and played an important role in the defence of the city. Most of the attacks came from the French and over the centuries reinforcements were added to improve it. Today you can still see the ramparts and cannons.

In 1794 the castle and the city fell into French hands. Since then the ownership of the castle has changed hands a number of times. In 1813 British soldiers joined the Spanish to fight against Napoleon. Many British soldiers were killed in the battle and are buried on the north hillside of Mount Urgull in the English Cemetery.

The *Sagrado Corazón* or Sacred Heart Statue is over twelve metres tall and stands on the highest point of Mount Urgull. It rests on a base that houses a chapel so the monument is actually twenty-four metres high. The statue created by Federico Coullaut was erected in 1950 and is also known as *Cristo de la Mota*. It can be seen by travellers on the sea four miles away.

Inside the castle there is a small museum known as *Casa de la Historia de Urgull* that uses models, artefacts and modern audio-visual technology to explain over eight hundred years of San Sebastián's history.

> *Walk north on Gaztelubide Kalea for 190 metres, turn right to stay on Gaztelubide Kalea for 300 metres then continue onto Monte Urgull Kalea for 60 metres.*
>
> *Bear a slight left to stay on Monte Urgull Kalea for 600 metres then turn left onto Pasealeku Berria. The Construcción Vacía will be on the left.*

Paseo Nuevo and the Construcción Vacía

The impressive steel sculpture located on the Paseo Nuevo, known as Construcción Vacía, the *Empty Construction*, is by the artist Jorge Oteiza. The work originally won an award at the Sao Paulo Biennale but this copy was placed here in 2002. The dramatic geometric silhouette is quite stunning when viewed against the gently curving coastline and sea.

The Paseo Nuevo or *New Walk* is a wonderful promenade that surrounds Mount Urgull running from the Old Town to the Aquarium. When the sea is rough it is a spectacular place from where to view the waves crashing against the promenade.

> *Continue to follow Pasealeku Berria around the coast for 250 metres until you reach Carl Blasco Imaz Plaza. Walk on over the plaza, take the stairs to the Aquarium.*

El Aquarium de San Sebastián

The aquarium of San Sebastián was the first natural science museum in Spain and was opened in 1925. Over the years there have been a number of changes but today it is divided into three sections. There is a huge pool known as *Oceanario* that has a tunnel going through it so you feel as though you are in the pool when you go through.

There are thematic aquariums with a diversity of fish from all over the world and also tactile aquariums where one can touch creatures such as starfish and sea urchins. The skeleton of a whale captured in 1878 makes an impressive display.

> *Walk across Kaiarriba Square onto Kaiko Pasealekua. The Naval Museum will be on the left.*

Museo Naval

The small Naval Museum located inside an old eighteenth century consulate house focuses on the tradition and history of the Basque maritime heritage. The exhibits are arranged on three floors. The first two floors are used to display various exhibits while the third has educational workshops and a library devoted to the naval history of the Basque country.

> *Walk on Kaiko Pasealekua for 260 metres to Kaimingaintxo Plaza then on for 230 metres. Turn left onto Lasta Plaza for 17 metres, right onto De Alderdi Eder Parkea for 14 metres then left onto Ijentea Kalea. San Sebastián City Hall will be on the right after 50 metres.*

Alderdi Eder Parkea and Ayuntamiento de San Sebastián

Alderdi Eder Parkea translates as *beautiful gardens* and they certainly are. Created in 1880 the gardens extend in front of the City Hall and La Concha Bay. Originally they held a circus, a velodrome and a theatre. Then in 1887 the casino was build.

There are benches to rest, small sculptures, a pond and some fountains. The garden has a variety of plants and flower beds lined with hedges and trees such as many tamarinds and elegant palm trees to give shade. The enormous merry-go-round in typical Belle Époque style is a huge attraction.

The majestic City Hall of San Sebastián was originally the casino. The casino was closed after a ban on gambling. The opening ceremony in 1924 for this magnificent building was attended by Queen Maria Christina of Austria. In the following years it hosted parties of the Belle Époque era for the aristocracy who spent their summers in San Sebastián.

In 1945 the City Council moved to this stunning building that had been adapted by the architects Alday and Arizmendi. The original City Hall was located in Constitution Square.

Ayuntamiento de San Sebastián

> Walk back south-west on Ijentea Kalea, turn left to follow De Alderdi Eder Parkea along the Alderdi Eder Park to the waterfront. At the end of the park you will see the Playa de La Concha.

Playa de La Concha

The Playa de La Concha or *Shell Beach* is one of the most beautiful beaches in Europe. Shaped like a shell this beach is the central beach in San Sebastián enclosed at one end by Mount Urgull and at the other by Mount Igueldo. The island of Santa Clara can be seen from this bay.

The spacious beach is 40 metres wide and 1350 metres long, bordered by a promenade for its entire length. After Queen María Cristina declared San Sebastián the *summer capital of Europe* it became fashionable with other aristocrats who built their lavish mansions along the shore.

As you walk along the beach you will pass many iconic buildings such as the Hotel Londres, La Perla and the Palacio Mirimar.

San Sebastián – Part 3

> *Walk along the promenade for about 600 metres. You will pass the Hotel Londres on the right. La Perla will be on the left.*

La Perla

In the early twentieth century when Queen María Cristina decided that San Sebastián was to be the royal summer home and other aristocrats visited too it was decided to build a wooden spa on La Concha beach. The Spa was replaced in 1912 by new premises that at the time were said to be the most beautiful in the world. At this time the promenade was widened and updated.

> *Cross both roads using the zebra crossings. Walk west on Mirakontxa Pasealekua for 230 metres then bear left to stay on this road. Continue for 450 metres then make a slight right for 220 metres. The Mirimar Palace and gardens will be on the left.*

Palacio de Mirimar and Jardines de Miramar

The Mirimar Palace was built in 1893 and commissioned by the Spanish Royal Family based on the ideas of the English architect Selden Wornum who also designed buildings in Biarritz and Saint Jean de Luz.

The building has a Queen Anne English cottage style with Neo-Gothic elements. It is built in sandstone and brick with additional timberwork. Although the palace has been renovated some of the rooms are as they were originally. These include the Royal Dining Room, the Petit Salon and the Music Hall among others. The master gardener Pierre Ducasse is responsible for the beautiful gardens.

When Queen María Cristina died Alfonso XIII inherited the palace but two years later it was confiscated by the government and became the residence for the President of the Republic when he visited the city. In Franco's time it was returned to the Royal family but in 1972 the local government bought it back as a public space so that everyone could enjoy the gardens although you cannot visit the palace.

Grand Houses Line the Promenade Along the Coast

> Walk north-west from the palace for 250 metres, turn right onto Mikelete Pasealekua. Use the zebra crossings and paths to cross the roads back to the beach.

Playa de Ondarreta

Ondarreta Beach is the smallest and most traditional beach in San Sebastián, a beautiful beach popular with the locals, families with children and wealthy visitors.

It is separated from Playa de la Concha by a rocky outcrop that becomes submerged when the tide comes in. Ondarreta is shorter than La Concha but much wider so there is more room when the tide comes in. There are showers, dressing rooms, sunbeds and umbrellas for rent as well as a small bar with refreshments.

> Walk west along the promenade for 270 metres. The statue of Maria Cristina will be on the left.

Estatua de María Cristina

The statue of Queen Maria Cristina stands in the Ondarreta gardens. The work by Madrid-born José Díaz Bueno was installed here in 1942 as a token of thanks to the much loved queen.

> *Walk to the end of the promenade. Use the zebra to cross Eduardo Chillida Pasealekua onto Satrustegi Hiribidea, turn left after 140 metres onto Plaza del Funicular. Follow it round to the ticket office for the funicular railway up to Mont Igueldo.*

Ferrocarril Funicular

The funicular railway has been taking visitors up and down Mount Igueldo since 1912. The funicular is a cog railway with wooden carriages, the oldest funicular railway in the Basque country and the third oldest in Spain. The station itself is an interesting building constructed from rustic stonework and timber with a mansard roof. Don't miss out on an opportunity to ride on the charismatic funicular as it ascends through the trees with glimpses of views below.

Funicular Railcar Making Its Way Up Mount Igueldo

View from Monte Igueldo

Monte Igueldo

At the top of the mountain the vintage fairground will remind you of past times with the wooden rollercoaster, trampolines and other peculiar attractions that are steeped in history.

Pay a visit to the Torreon de Igueldo which was a fortified lighthouse reconstructed from a sixteenth century tower. It no longer works as a new lighthouse replaced it in 1854 but inside the tower is an exhibition of the customs and life of San Sebastián citizens.

Before you leave take time to stand on the balcony and gaze out across the wonderful city of San Sebastián. Nowhere in the city will you get better views than here. They are just spectacular. You can pick out places you have visited and really appreciate what a wonderful city this is.

Final Thoughts

These tours were written in response to guided tours that the author attended whilst in the Basque Country, all of which tended to rush the participants from one location to the next and only included the most popular tourist sights. The walks in this book were designed to introduce you to the charms of this region while exploring five towns and cities in France and Spain. They will have taken you to a range of attractions to give a balanced view of each place.

By visiting these towns and cities you will understand how location played such a vital role in their history and why the Basque culture is so important to its people. You will have seen evidence of how the members of Royalty taking their holidays in these places influenced their growth.

In Bayonne you will have seen not only the medieval fortifications but also the pretty houses that line the banks of the rivers and appreciate how the city has worked hard to preserve its heritage. Biarritz will have charmed with its eclectic architecture incorporating a mixture of historic styles as well as its stunning coastline.

In Hendaye you will again have seen fortifications and evidence of the wars between France and Spain as you walk along the bay, been charmed by the houses of Neo-Basque style and hopefully the impressive Chateau.

You will have appreciated why Hondarribia is thought to be one of the most beautiful towns in the Basque Country with its rich architecture, history and gastronomy. San Sebastián too is a magnificent town with three impressive sandy beaches, famed throughout the world for its Pintxos and Belle Époque architecture.

There may not be time to explore the interior of every building or visit all museums included in each day's walking tour so a section for your own notes is included over the next few pages. Here you may wish to make notes of places to visit if you have any spare time on another day, or intend to return to the Basque Country in the future. You may also wish to write down things such as restaurants where you have enjoyed traditional Basque food or favourite attractions that you can pass onto friends.

Notes

Also from PS Quick

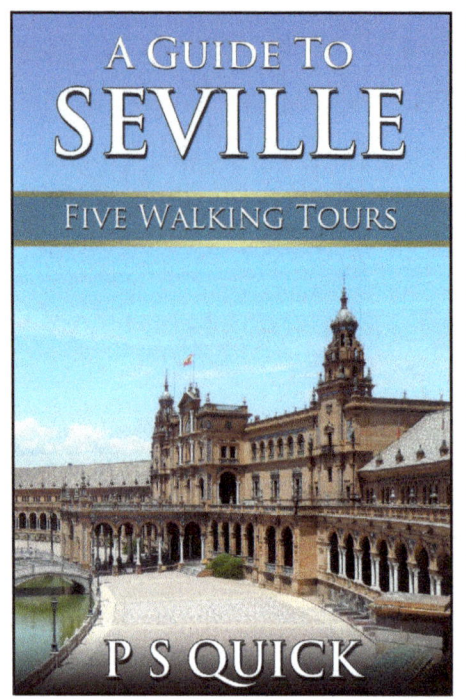

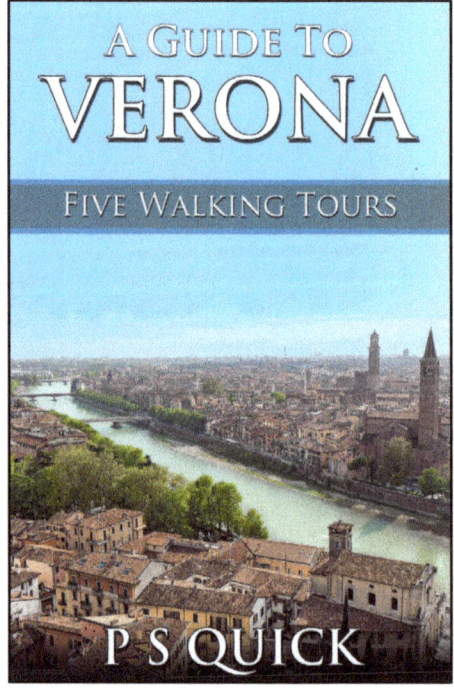

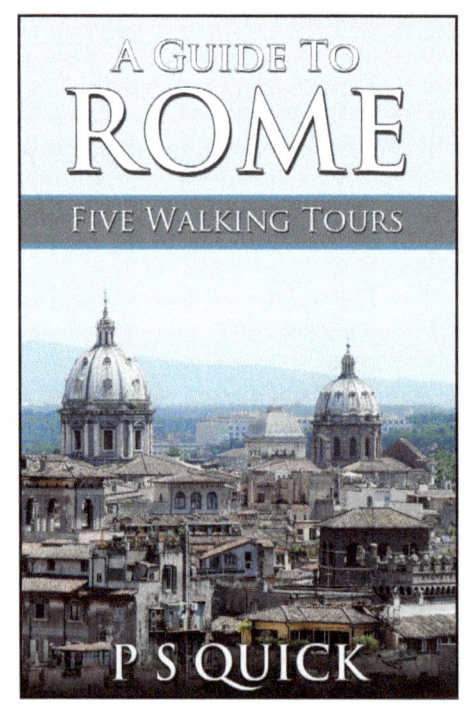

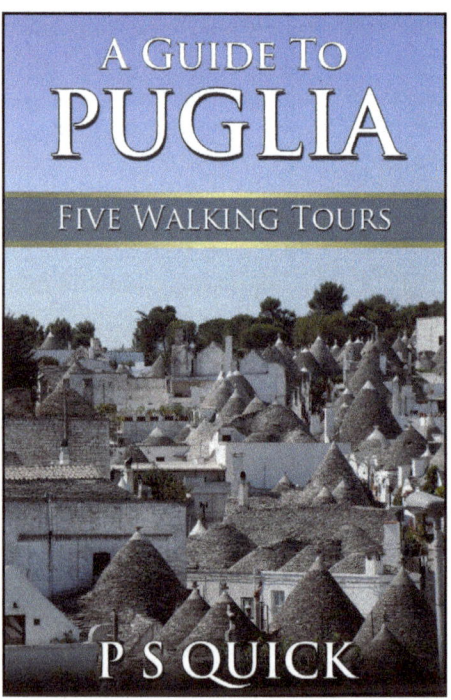